I0048645

Copyright

Part of the sales from this book and others by the author go towards creating **scholarships** for students, such as one specifically for those with **disabilities**. So please do not plagiarize this book.

The author absolves themselves of any liability related to the use of this book.

ISBN (KDP Amazon) 9798863681917
ISBN (paperback): 978-1-7358165-4-8
ISBN (digital): 978-1-7358165-3-1

Author: Carlynn Greene
Publisher: Carlynn Greene
Editor: Tyra Brooks
Fact-Checker: Tyra Brooks
www.scholarship-guru.com

Dedication

This book is dedicated to the Clayton family, my brother Quenton, all the students, parents, educators, disability advocates, and healthcare professionals out there.

Disclaimer

All information provided is dated as of October 2023. Some of the information seen throughout this book is prone to changing over time due to amendments to legislation, rules, terms, and eligibility criteria. To be provided with the most up-to-date information, please refer to your state's resources as seen on their website, and personally consult with related professionals. Although this book is very detailed, it is still not all-encompassing with the information provided, but rather a starting point in an effort to make this entire process less overwhelming and more structured. It should not be used as your only reference material, so please do external research and outreach as well.

Table of Contents

Scholarship Guru Success Stories

"You have trained me and Tyler well and we appreciate it. They are rolling in. He had to stop applying because Tyler is tired of interviews, and we have enough money now so someone else can get some."
- *Clayton family*
- *11x scholarship winner during senior year of high school*
- *Receives educational funding from a disability program*
- *Condition: ADHD*

"Scholarship #24 came in earlier this week - one specific to my program. I can't believe I was able to win something so late in my senior year (of college), and it was a complete surprise! This now brings me up to $60,750 in total, which helps me so much as I focus on graduation this August!"
- *Mary Glossop*
- *Graduated debt-free in 2023*
- *Condition: Dairy & stomach-related*

"I started my scholarship journey nearing the end of my first year of graduate school. I recently won the Taco Bell Live Mas scholarship. It was unexpected! Pretty shocked and surprised that I won my first-ever scholarship!"
- *Anshu Choudhary*
- *Condition: Autism spectrum*

Scholarship-Guru.com winners

$103,000 $56,500 $60,000 $120,000 $68,000

$60,000 Full-Tuition Full-Ride $50,500 $60,750

Legitimacy / Credibility

Whenever I share about my business that helps students obtain financial aid, I typically receive positive feedback. However, there are others who automatically assume that it is a "scam" or "not legit."

I have never claimed that with my advice a student is "100% guaranteed" to receive financial aid or be admitted into a school. If I were to say that, then yes, that would be dishonest.

In addition, I am a journalist. I previously worked at the national level as a news producer for ABC News (which is owned by Disney). Journalism is heavily dependent on research, writing skills, transparency, and legitimacy.

My goal is to simply try and make higher education more financially accessible and teach other ways to save money in general.

My work has been nationally recognized by LinkedIn and TikTok, and I received business grants from both companies ranging from $15,000 to $50,000. In 2021 I won the ADCOLOR TikTok Creator Award for my scholarship content that promotes diversity and inclusion.

If you would like to hear from students I have helped or learn more about what I do, then feel free to view the links below.

- **<u>Winner testimonies</u>**
- **<u>News coverage</u>**

Why I Started Helping Others

What started me on this journey of helping others with college financial aid (and other ways to save money) was my mother. During my senior year of high school, I won a scholarship from a hospital where I had been volunteering for years. I remember being woken up by my mother crying at my bedside. She was on her knees shaking and thanking God over and over again. In her hand was the award letter for the scholarship that I won from the hospital.

That was when I realized that the knowledge I have about financial aid shouldn't be kept to myself. From there on out, I had a responsibility to help students and parents — after all, many parents also bear the financial burden of paying for higher education.

The First Time Someone Told Me They Won

The first time a student told me they won a scholarship was in 2017 via email. Not only was this student the first one to tell me they won, but they were also not from the U.S. — they were from the D.R. Congo, studying in Ghana on a full ride. Years later, that same student notified me about another fully funded award he received to study abroad in the United Kingdom for his graduate studies.

When reading his message, I couldn't help but cry.

It felt like an out-of-body experience. It is surreal that the advice that I had filmed in my parents' bedroom — reached across the ocean. Even with a cheap camera, beginner editing skills, and a hint of imposter syndrome, I was able to change not only his life — but also the thousands of students who reported their winning results thereafter.

That's when I knew that what I was doing — was groundbreaking.

Preface

How I went through the "5 Stages of Grief" when I learned about the main opportunity you will learn about in this book:

Stage 1: Denial -
When I initially heard about the main lesser-known resource that inspired this book, I was both shocked and confused.

A mother in my scholarship **program** titled, *The Scholarship Algorithm* (where I teach people my step-by-step strategies that enabled me to win 30x scholarships for undergraduate and graduate school) — was the one who told me about it. Her son had already won **$246,000 in scholarships** after participating in my program. However, with his condition (ADHD) he also qualified for a **fully funded** undergraduate college education through a government assistance program. It offered to fully cover tuition, books, housing, transportation, and technology (such as a new laptop).

Literally *everything*.

When she first told me, I couldn't wrap my head around this. *As a financial aid coach since 2017 — why am I **now** just learning about this?*

Here I was, the "teacher" being taught about a game-changing resource for students with disabilities.

The more information the mother shared with me, the more confused I became.

First, was the terminology. The official name of it didn't indicate anything related to education. I searched for keywords within the informational PDFs she sent, and again, nothing indicated *college, university, trade school,* or let alone the words *student* or *education*. I later learned that the keyword I should have been looking for was **training** which can extend to **educational training**.

I initially avoided learning more about it because everything seemed so complex. The information and wording on their official websites felt like I was walking into a crowded house with a terrible layout.

Why is there a bed in the kitchen? Why is there carpet in the bathroom? Why is the clothing closet in the garage?

Why is a resource that is supposed to make things more accessible for those with disabilities — not very clear with how it communicates this information?

Stage 2: Anger -
The more I learned about this resource and how few knew about it, the more frustrated I became.

The National Center for Education Statistics, (**NCES**), found that 19% of undergraduate students report having a disability. Additionally, a research **study** reported that the average federal student loan debt among graduates with disabilities is approximately $27,490. Also, whenever a student with a disability or their parent reached out to me to learn about financial aid, I would ask them if they knew about this government program, and almost 100% of the time their answer was — "no."

Let's say that in an alternate universe, every person with a disability or health condition knew about this program and actually applied it. Many applicants would be selected. However, not every person would be selected because funding opportunities are limited. Even so, the simple gesture of more people knowing and applying could have a drastic effect on curving the student loan debt crisis amongst those with disabilities.

What really sent me over the edge was learning that this resource has existed for not just a couple of years ... or recently introduced in the 21st century ... but it has been around **since September of 1973.** I published this book in October of 2023.

That's **50 years,** *five decades, half a century* of thousands if not millions of students with disabilities not knowing about this specific resource and its educational benefits.

This made me even more livid.

Stage 3: Bargaining -
I tried to find meaning in this. *Why isn't this advertised more?*

I reached out to the mother I mentioned earlier who's in my scholarship program. I needed to vent. *How very professional of me, right?*

During our call, I informed her that I was going to write a book about this entire process specifically relating to its student benefit. In addition, researching and organizing a plethora of other helpful resources for those with disabilities to save money.

She was elated and stressed how much it was needed. She then told me she spoke with another parent at her son's university and the topic came up. They knew about it, informed her, and later she informed me.

And now, I'm informing **you**.

She was in the right place at the right time. I can't help but imagine if that conversation hadn't come up. Her son would still be going to college debt-free via scholarships and grants even without the government program for those with disabilities — *but what about* **you guys?**

Who knows? Maybe we would have gone another 50 years with the majority of people who in fact are eligible for this government program never knowing and instead having student loan debt.

Stage 4: Depression -
I started to feel guilty.

I've been helping students win scholarships and obtain other forms of financial aid for years. However, about 1 in 5 of those students have some sort of medical condition. I could have made so much more of an impact had I known about this earlier. The goal and slogan I use often is — *Less owing **loans**. More owning **scholarships**.* I felt ashamed that I couldn't have helped more people with realizing this goal despite being a "Scholarship Guru."

I'm supposed to know everything and anything related to this process ... *right?*

I can't help but think about another student in my scholarship program, a graduate school student on the Autism spectrum. He won his first-ever scholarship. A partial scholarship that was highly competitive with thousands of applicants across the nation. He also got a nationally competitive internship learning from my program as well!

However, this process was far from easy — we had to go through *five rounds of revisions* to his scholarship application video before submitting it.

When it comes to scholarships and other competitive applications, you have to market yourself and present a certain way to grab people's attention and stand out. However, many on the Autism spectrum might have difficulty recognizing certain social cues and knowing when to adjust to suit different social circumstances.

That scholarship he won ended up being his first and last.

He's still trying to pay off his graduate school student loans. He could have utilized the opportunity that I will teach you in this book to fund his graduate education as well.

And while my program has helped students with and without disabilities win scholarships — this government program specifically for those with disabilities could have been a better deal for them. After all, it caters to their needs specifically while being monitored by someone who specializes in working with those who have medical conditions.

Stage 5: Acceptance -

If I could turn back time, I would tell every student I have mentored about this. However, that is not possible. What I can do now is take the steps necessary to ensure that countless students know about this opportunity and apply for it.

I hope that my huge platform on social media (amassing over 950,000 followers across socials) and the teachings of this book can make this possible.

Outside of teaching through this book and spreading awareness through social media, I plan to push for change at the legislative level. I already have plans to do so as it relates to scholarships. I outlined this as one of my missions within my application that got me a scholarship from the U.S. Congress's Congressional Black Caucus. This would simply be an extension of that effort.

With that being said — you will find towards the end of this book a **Change.org petition** I have made. The goal is to grab the attention of our political leaders into streamlining this entire process so that it is more accessible for others to apply to as well.

Now that I have gone through the 5 Stages of Grief — *it's time to teach.*

Introduction

There are various ways for individuals with disabilities / health conditions to obtain a higher education at a fraction of the usual cost — if not completely for free. Some are government-funded, and others are privately-funded.

In this book, you will learn many methods. I have broken them down into four parts to easily navigate and refer back to. It's outlined as follows:

- **Part 1:** The Qualifying Round - required criteria, becoming eligible, the various benefits, and more
- **Part 2:** The Application Phase - how to stand out with your application, interview hacks, and more
- **Part 3:** The Inducted Stage - once accepted, what to expect in the beginning and throughout
- **Part 4:** The Alternative Steps - scholarships, grants, money saving hacks, resources, and more

Additionally, with this book it's important to note that many of the resources and advice mentioned can be beneficial for not only students with disabilities based in the United States, but also:

- Parents with disabilities
- Individuals in general with disabilities, such as those who are not interested in higher education
- People outside of the U.S. with disabilities
- Those without disabilities

Unfortunately, many of the opportunities and resources seen within this book are not very well known due to:

- A lack of advertisement
- Complex wording or legal jargon
- Clunky and disorganized websites that overwhelm visitors on where to start

This book hopes to bridge the gap in learning.

The Disabled Debt-Free Degree

My background —
As a brief introduction, my name is Carlynn Greene and I am a **30x scholarship winner.** I have had the privilege of being **debt-free** for both my **undergraduate and graduate school studies.**

Over the years, I have helped a multitude of students win millions in scholarships, including students on the Autism spectrum, those with ADHD, and so forth.

However, the me from 10 years ago never would have envisioned where I am now.

I originally aspired to be a doctor — a nephrologist specializing in kidney care. I was inspired by my older brother's medical condition. He is what many would call a "miracle." The doctors said he wouldn't make it, but he will be turning 30-years-old soon. The Make-A-Wish Foundation even came to our house and built two tree houses in the backyard for him and gifted our family with a trip to Disney World. He even missed the first day of grade school to get a kidney transplant and is currently on dialysis since that donated kidney expired. Our family hopes that he can get back on the kidney donor list soon.

Due to my brother's condition, I was determined to go to medical school. However, I eventually learned that I had a strong aversion to blood. There's actually an official term for this — *Hemophobia*. When I see a lot of blood in-person my hands start to shake, and I feel dizzy. Oddly enough, I don't have the same reaction to blood seen on TV or in video games.

I suspect that this came as a result of seeing my brother in pain so much that over time this condition developed. Of course, a medical doctor has to be comfortable around blood and should have stable hands to be a surgeon. I tried to overcome this — but couldn't no matter what.

A change in career plans was necessary. Eventually, I began studying journalism because of my passion for writing, researching, and interest in informing others via media platforms.

I previously worked as a producer for ABC News Live. I am a contributor for certain news outlets and report about college and financial aid as an extension of my career in journalism.

Even though I couldn't be a doctor, I have helped future doctors, nurses, immunologists, biomedical engineers, and medical laboratory scientists to obtain funding for their education. I live vicariously through the students in the healthcare field and other pathways alike.

That's why I do not regret or wish my journey was any different. Everything happens for a reason. Rejection is redirection and you can turn pain into purpose.

I like to think of this book as a full-circle moment to what I originally thought my future would consist of. At first, I wanted to help those with medical conditions as a doctor, but now I can do so as an author.

Now that that's been established — it's time to advance to the first chapter of this book which is hopefully the first chapter towards your debt-free journey and beyond!

Accessing Links Mentioned

Throughout this book, I will refer to various online resources for you to use. If you are reading the **physical version of the book**, of course typing all those URL links can be very time-consuming. That is why I made sure to provide a resource that has all the links mentioned **within one master document**.

You will find this in the **"Reference Info" chapter on page 134.**

Also, to know which links will be in the master link document, you will know if that link is BOTH **bolded AND underlined.**

PART 1: The Qualifying Round - required criteria, becoming eligible, the various benefits, definitions, and more

The Disabled Debt-Free Degree

By: Carlynn D. Greene

Disability Statistics in the U.S.

Students with disabilities tend to graduate college or high school at significantly lower rates than people without disabilities.

A research **study** titled *Above-Average Student Loan Debt for Students with Disabilities Attending Postsecondary Institutions* found that "the average federal student loan debt among graduates with disabilities is approximately $27,490" (Bullington et al., 2022, p. 7).

That same study found that students with disabilities attending private universities had approximately $13,053 more in federal student loan debt than public university students. And for military veterans with disabilities, they owe $4,806 less than disabled students who are not veterans.

According to a survey conducted by **Pew Charitable Trusts**, "Borrowers who reported ever having a disability were significantly more likely to experience default (50%) than those without a disability (33%)." Earlier **research** indicates that borrowers with disabilities may face lower incomes and higher unemployment rates which could make affording payments difficult (Mitra et al., 2014).

In terms of how many students within the United States have reported disabilities, the data is as follows. According to the National Center for Education Statistics (**NCES**), 19% of undergraduate students report having a disability.

Also, **data** from NCES for the 2021-2022 academic year, reported that approximately 15% of all public-school students in the United States received special education services under the Individuals with Disabilities Education Act (IDEA).

List of Disabilities / Health Conditions

There are many different types of disabilities out there. Here is a list of some types with examples.

- **Mental Health Disabilities**: Including conditions like depression, anxiety disorders, bipolar disorder, or schizophrenia that may affect a person's ability to work.
- **Physical Disabilities**: Such as mobility impairments, muscular disorders (such as arthritis, carpal tunnel, etc.), cerebral palsy, amputations, and other conditions that affect physical functioning.
- **Chronic Health Conditions**: Such as asthma and other respiratory types, vitiligo and other skin types, allergies, chronic pain, fibromyalgia, chronic fatigue syndrome (CFS), and autoimmune disorders that affect daily functioning.
- **Sensory Disabilities**: Including visual impairments (blindness, low vision) and hearing impairments (deafness, hard of hearing).
- **Neurodevelopmental / Neurodivergent Disabilities**: Including autism spectrum disorder (ASD), attention-deficit/hyperactivity disorder (ADHD), attention deficit disorder (ADD), and Tourette syndrome.
- **Intellectual Disabilities**: Such as developmental delays or intellectual challenges that impact learning and adaptive functioning.
- **Neurological Disabilities**: Such as traumatic brain injuries (TBI), multiple sclerosis (MS), severe migraines, having frequent seizures (such as with epilepsy) that impact cognitive and neurological functioning.
- **Learning Disabilities**: Such as dyslexia, dyspraxia, dyscalculia, or processing disorders that affect academic and vocational skills.
- **Psychiatric Disabilities**: Including conditions such as post-traumatic stress disorder (PTSD), obsessive-compulsive disorder (OCD), or major depressive disorder.

Invisible vs. Visible Disabilities

Invisible disabilities and visible disabilities refer to whether a person's disability is readily apparent to others or not. Here's a comparison between the two:

Invisible Disabilities:
- **Definition**: Conditions or impairments that are not immediately evident from a person's outward appearance.
- **Examples**: Chronic pain, fibromyalgia, chronic fatigue syndrome, mental health conditions (such as anxiety, depression, or PTSD), epilepsy, certain learning disabilities, and autoimmune disorders.
- **Challenges**: Those with invisible disabilities may have trouble obtaining accommodations or understanding from others. This can lead to misconceptions or skepticism from others about the legitimacy of their condition. Therefore, self-advocacy and having others to advocate on their behalf is especially important and can help with verifying their status.

Visible Disabilities:
- **Definition**: Conditions or impairments that are apparent to others upon observation.
- **Examples**: Physical disabilities like amputations, mobility impairments, visual impairments with guide dogs or canes, and hearing impairments with the use of hearing aids or sign language.
- **Challenges**: While visible disabilities may be easier to recognize, they can also face challenges related to stereotypes, discrimination, and misconceptions about their abilities and capacities.

Addiction as a Disability?

The classification of drug and alcohol addiction as a disability can vary depending on the context and the specific laws or regulations of a country. In the United States, drug and alcohol addiction may be considered a disability under **certain circumstances**. The Americans with Disabilities Act (ADA) prohibits discrimination against individuals with disabilities in areas like public accommodations, and government services.

The ADA defines a disability as a physical or mental impairment that substantially limits one or more major life activities, including major bodily functions. Substance disorders like addiction to drugs or alcohol can be considered impairments under the ADA.

However, it's important to note that the ADA does **not protect** individuals who are **currently** engaging in the **illegal use of drugs.** The ADA explicitly excludes individuals who are currently using illegal drugs from the definition of disability. It is also important to **mention** that individuals in recovery or who have successfully completed a rehabilitation program might be protected under the ADA.

The Rehabilitation Act explicitly states that individuals who are currently engaging in the illegal use of drugs are **not considered eligible** for the government program this book will cover.

Again, this is for the U.S. specifically. In other countries, the recognition of drug and alcohol addiction as a disability and the extent of legal protections also varies. Some countries may have specific disability laws that include or exclude substance use disorders as disabilities.

Additionally, not every single drug type may be considered for this government program — so make sure to talk to the right specialist in your specific state as it may vary.

Finally, if you or someone you know is considering the program this book will cover, it's advisable to contact the disability agency in your state to inquire about eligibility and support available.

Don't Fake a Disability

The documentary, *Operation Varsity Blues,* on Netflix exposed a scheme where wealthy parents paid large sums of money to cheat the college admissions process.

One of the methods used was falsifying having a disability.

They hired a psychiatrist who provided fake diagnoses of learning disabilities or other conditions to justify the need for extended time or other special accommodations during standardized tests.

Faking disabilities or exaggerating impairments for personal benefit takes advantage of the accommodations meant to support individuals with disabilities. It can lead to reduced resources and opportunities for those who genuinely need them.

As a result of the actions of those parents, there were:
- **Legal Consequences**: Many of the parents involved in the scandal faced legal repercussions. Some pleaded guilty, while others went to trial and were convicted.
- **Criminal Convictions**: Several individuals, including parents and college coaches, received prison sentences for their involvement in fraudulent activities. Some sentences were for a few months and others faced several years in prison.
- **Loss of Reputation**: The scandal significantly damaged the reputation of the involved colleges and universities, as it exposed vulnerabilities in the college admissions process. Some coaches and school administrators were fired or resigned due to their involvement.
- **Impact on Students**: Students whose parents engaged in fraudulent activities faced social and emotional consequences, including embarrassment and stigma. In some cases, they were expelled from the universities they had fraudulently gained admission to.

With that being said, if perhaps you are reading this book with the intent to use the advice seen to get you or for your child's education to be free or cheaper — but the student in question does not have any disability — then please think otherwise. **It's unethical.**

Instead, pass this book along to someone who does have a disability and could benefit from the information provided.

If you want to learn about other forms of financial aid for **students without a disability,** then check out any of my **free trainings** and downloadable resources on my website, **scholarship-guru.com.**

Finally, for those who are **not formally diagnosed yet** the next chapter will be covering how to get diagnosed for free or at a reduced price. Having this documentation is **mandatory** for what I will be teaching throughout most of this book.

Getting Diagnosed for Free or Cheaper

Many people have a disability but never get officially diagnosed due to:
- Social stigmas relating to disabilities
- Not thinking that their condition is serious enough to do so
- Settling with self-diagnosing themselves
- The cost of getting diagnosed

For instance, the cost to test for ADHD can range anywhere from a couple of hundred dollars to thousands. The amount varies depending on location, who does the test, how comprehensive the test is, etc.

There are free platforms that can help you with determining — as a starting point — if you have a certain condition such as **WebMD Symptom Checker** and the **Mayo Clinic Symptom Checker**.

However, the main program I will be covering in this book requires **official documentation of a disability** from a qualified healthcare professional or licensed diagnostician. Additionally, many of the scholarships and grants seen throughout this book to assist with the cost of higher education, medical treatment, or assistive technology tend to also require proof of having a disability as well.

Getting diagnosed for a medical condition for free or at a lower cost can be challenging, but there are some options available that may help reduce expenses —
- **Public Health Clinics:** Many public health clinics offer low-cost or free medical services, including diagnostics and consultations. Check with your local health department or community health centers to see if they provide the services you need.
- **University Hospitals and Clinics:** Some university-affiliated hospitals and medical schools offer discounted or sliding-scale fees for medical services. Medical students, under the supervision of licensed professionals, may conduct evaluations and diagnostics.
- **Telemedicine Services:** Online telemedicine platforms may offer more affordable options for medical consultations and diagnostics, depending on your location and the services required.

- **Nonprofit Organizations:** Some nonprofit organizations and charities offer medical assistance programs for specific conditions. Look for organizations that focus on the condition you suspect you may have and inquire about diagnostic services they may provide.
- **Free Health Screenings:** Periodically, community events and health fairs offer free health screenings, including screenings for specific conditions. These events may be a good opportunity to get preliminary assessments.
- **Medicaid or Low-Income Health Programs**: If you meet income eligibility criteria, you may qualify for Medicaid or other low-income health programs that provide coverage for medical evaluations and treatments.
- **Clinical Trials:** Some research studies and clinical trials may offer free medical evaluations for specific conditions. However, participation in clinical trials should be carefully considered and discussed with healthcare professionals.
- **Patient Assistance Programs**: Some pharmaceutical companies offer patient assistance programs that provide free or discounted medications, which may be relevant if a diagnosis requires specific tests or treatments.
- **Sliding-Scale Clinics**: Some private medical clinics operate on a sliding-scale fee basis, where fees are adjusted based on the patient's ability to pay.
- **Local Charities and Foundations:** Some local charities or foundations may offer medical assistance or financial aid for specific conditions.
- **Vocational Rehabilitation (VR) Programs:** This can potentially cover the cost of diagnosing disabilities or medical conditions when it is necessary to determine eligibility for VR services. However, keep in mind that the turn-around-time to help cover the cost may be delayed due to:
  - The complexity of the disability
  - The availability of healthcare professionals
  - The workload of the VR agency (such as if they have a lot of applicants)
  - The specific policies of the VR program in your state or country.

Remember to **verify** the legitimacy and credentials of any healthcare provider or organization you choose for diagnostic services. If you are concerned about your ability to afford medical evaluations, discussing your situation with potential providers and exploring available options may help you find a solution that suits your needs and financial circumstances.

Finally, try to schedule **getting diagnosed a few months before** you start your application for the government assistance program this book covers.

Important Definitions

Under the Americans with Disabilities Act (**ADA**), "An individual with a disability is defined by the ADA as a person who has a physical or mental impairment that substantially limits one or more major life activities, a person who has a history or record of such an impairment (even if they do not currently have it), or a person who is **perceived** by others as having such an impairment."

Vocational Rehabilitation (VR) Program is a specialized program that aims to assist individuals with disabilities in preparing for, obtaining, maintaining, or advancing in meaningful and gainful employment. The primary goal of VR services is to empower individuals with disabilities to achieve greater independence and economic self-sufficiency through employment opportunities.

VR is a comprehensive and individualized process that involves assessment, counseling, guidance, training, and other support services to help individuals with disabilities overcome barriers to employment.

According to the **Vocational Rehabilitation Administration**, the federal government provides 78.7% of the total VR program cost, and individual states are responsible for contributing the remaining 21.3% as their financial match.

VR services are provided by state and federal agencies in many countries (*they may take on a different name in other nations*). These agencies work collaboratively with disabled individuals to create an **Individualized Plan for Employment (IPE).** The plan outlines the necessary services / steps to achieve the individual's vocational goals.

A **504 coordinator** — also known as a **504 counselor** — is a designated staff member at an institution (often the school counselor) responsible for overseeing the implementation of Section 504 of the Rehabilitation Act of 1973. This law prohibits discrimination based on disability in any program or activity receiving federal financial assistance. These counselors work with students, teachers, and parents to develop personalized accommodations to help students with disabilities be successful academically and with school activities.

Next, I want to discuss the **Individuals with Disabilities Education Act (IDEA)**, which is a federal law in the United States that ensures access to a free and appropriate public education for children with disabilities. IDEA outlines the rights and protections for students with disabilities and requires schools to provide individualized special education services. At the same time, allowing them to access educational opportunities and reach their full potential.

As mentioned earlier in this book, **data** from NCES for the 2021-2022 academic year, reported that approximately 15% of all public-school students in the United States received special education services under the IDEA.

VR vs. WIOA

The Workforce Innovation and Opportunity Act (WIOA) and Vocational Rehabilitation (VR) are two distinct but closely related programs that aim to support individuals in achieving their employment and career goals. Here's how WIOA and VR are connected:

- **Eligibility and Target Population:**
  - WIOA serves both those with disabilities AND those without disabilities.
  - VR is specifically for those with disabilities.
- **Education and Training:**
  - Both WIOA and VR provide support for education and training to help participants develop the skills and qualifications needed for employment.
  - WIOA offers various programs, including on-the-job training, higher education training, and skills training.
  - VR may also fund higher education and training such as for college and trade school.
- **Individualized Plans:** Both WIOA and VR utilize individualized planning processes.
  - Under WIOA, there is a focus on creating Individual Employment Plans (IEPs) or Individual Service Strategies (ISS), which are individualized plans designed to support participants in achieving their vocational goals.
  - For VR, individuals work with their VR counselors to develop Individualized Plans for Employment (IPEs), which outline their vocational goals and the services necessary to reach those goals. IPEs tend to be more customized and individualized in comparison.
- **Coordination of Services:** WIOA and VR programs often collaborate and coordinate services to maximize the effectiveness of workforce development efforts for individuals with disabilities. This collaboration includes sharing resources, avoiding duplication of services, and leveraging each program's strengths to better serve participants.
- **Collaboration with Employers:** Both WIOA and VR emphasize collaboration with employers to promote job placements.

VR vs. VR&E

For those who are somewhat familiar with VR, perhaps they mainly associate it with being a resource for those in the military. However, apart from veterans, this program is also available for individuals with disabilities who are not affiliated with the military. For both VR and VR&E they have the educational training benefit available, whether that is to pursue an associate's, bachelor's, master's degree, etc. However — not everyone who applies will be selected for either program.

For clarification of terminology:
- **VR Program:** Vocational Rehabilitation helps individuals with disabilities prepare for, obtain, or maintain employment. VR services are offered by VR agencies and are **not** specific to only veterans. Even so, veterans are still welcome to apply as well.
- **VR&E Program:** The Veteran Readiness and Employment program is for U.S. veterans specifically. As outlined within Chapter 31 of the Vocational Rehabilitation Program, this is a comprehensive program provided by the U.S. Department of Veterans Affairs (VA) to assist disabled veterans and service members with achieving their employment and vocational goals.
    - For more on VR&E eligibility, use this **link**.
    - To apply for VR&E, use this **link.**
    - Here is a helpful **YouTube Playlist** by @NickTheVet who walks you through the VR&E process as a veteran. Most of her channel's videos are dedicated to VR&E, so definitely check them out!
    - @NickTheVet also has **scripts** to use to petition for VR&E benefits if rejected.

Additionally, a veteran might choose to use the general Vocational Rehabilitation (VR) services instead of the Veteran Readiness and Employment (VR&E) program for various reasons.

Here are some scenarios where a **veteran might opt for general VR:**
- **Eligibility Criteria:** Not all veterans may meet the specific eligibility criteria for the VR&E Program. The VR&E Program requires a **service-connected disability** and an employment handicap, so if a veteran's disability is not service-connected,

they may not be eligible for VR&E but could still be eligible for general VR services based on other disability criteria.

- ○ The U.S. Department of **Veteran Affairs** defines a **service-connected condition** as an illness or injury that was caused by — or got worse because of — your active military service.

- **Scope of Services:** The VR&E Program primarily focuses on helping veterans prepare for and obtain employment. If a veteran's vocational goals involve non-employment-related objectives, such as independent living skills or pursuing educational opportunities unrelated to employment, they might find that general VR services offer a more suitable approach to meeting their needs.

- **Level of Support Needed:** The VR&E Program is designed to provide comprehensive vocational rehabilitation services tailored to the unique challenges faced by disabled veterans transitioning to civilian employment. If a veteran's vocational goals are relatively straightforward, and they require minimal support or accommodations, they may find that general VR services can adequately meet their needs.

- **State-Specific Factors:** Each state's vocational rehabilitation agency may have different services and resources available. In some cases, a veteran might find that the general VR services offered in their state align better with their individual needs and goals.

How it All Started

The roots of VR and WIOA can be traced back to the early 20th century, when efforts were made to provide vocational training and support to individuals with disabilities, particularly veterans of wars. Here's a history overview:

World War I Era: The vocational rehabilitation movement gained significant momentum after World War I. During this time, there was an increased awareness of the need to support injured soldiers returning from war. Vocational training centers were established to help veterans with disabilities acquire new skills and reenter the workforce.

Smith-Fess Act of 1920: In the United States, the first federal legislation related to vocational rehabilitation was the Smith-Fess Act of 1920 (also known as the Civilian Vocational Rehabilitation Act). This act provided funding for vocational rehabilitation services for civilians with disabilities.

World War II and the Vocational Rehabilitation Amendments of 1943: The demand for vocational rehabilitation services grew during and after World War II. In response, the U.S. Congress passed the Vocational Rehabilitation Amendments of 1943, which expanded the scope of vocational rehabilitation services and included specific provisions for individuals with disabilities resulting from the war.

The Rehabilitation Act of 1973: This landmark legislation prohibited discrimination against individuals with disabilities and established comprehensive vocational rehabilitation services through Title I. It also created the framework for the establishment of state vocational rehabilitation agencies in the United States.

As it relates to education, **section 504** of the Rehabilitation Act is applicable to any establishment, whether private or public, that receives federal funding for any of its programs or services. This implies that any educational institution receiving federal funds must adhere to the provisions of Section 504 to ensure equal access and non-discrimination for students with disabilities.

The Disabled Debt-Free Degree

The Americans with Disabilities Act (ADA) of 1990: The ADA was a major milestone in disability rights, prohibiting discrimination against individuals with disabilities in various areas of public life, including employment and in education. The ADA reinforced the importance of vocational rehabilitation services in promoting equal opportunities for individuals with disabilities in the workplace. The ADA and Section 504 safeguard students by prohibiting discrimination based on disability within educational establishments.

These laws encompass various facets, such as admissions, housing, programming (such as extracurricular activities), and other provisions. Educational establishments are obligated to provide necessary modifications or accommodations for students with disabilities who require them.

The ADA pertains to both public and private establishments — **except** for those affiliated with religious organizations or religious schools and some **other** categories as well. Specifically, Title II of the ADA relates to state-funded schools, including universities, community colleges, and vocational schools. Whereas Title III of the ADA encompasses private colleges and vocational / trade schools.

The Workforce Innovation and Opportunity Act (WIOA): The Workforce Innovation and Opportunity Act (WIOA) was signed into law on July 22, 2014, and it became effective on July 1, 2015. It is federal legislation that reauthorized and replaced the previous workforce development law, the Workforce Investment Act (WIA). As it relates to Vocational Rehabilitation (VR), the Rehabilitation Act of 1973 was reauthorized and amended by WIOA in 2014.

WIOA made significant amendments that govern the VR program today.

For instance, WIOA introduced several changes to the VR program, including the establishment of Pre-Employment Transition Services (Pre-ETS) for students with disabilities. These services are designed to provide early support and career exploration opportunities for students with disabilities to help them transition successfully from school to postsecondary education or employment.

VR - Why Don't Many Know About It?

There are several reasons why many people may not be familiar with VR programs.

- **Word Choice**: The term "Vocational Rehabilitation" (VR) can be a bit misleading in terms of its association with paying for college expenses. The word "vocational" often implies job-focused or career-oriented training. As a result, many individuals may not immediately associate VR with financial assistance for college education.
- **Lack of Awareness**: VR programs are not as widely promoted or advertised as some other government assistance programs — despite being around for over 50 years now. As a result, many individuals with disabilities may not be aware that such services exist to help them with their employment goals.
- **Limited Outreach**: VR agencies may have limited resources for outreach and public awareness campaigns. As a result, they may struggle to reach and inform all the eligible individuals who could benefit from their services.
- **Stigma and Misconceptions**: Some people with disabilities may be hesitant to seek help from VR programs due to stigmas associated with disabilities or misconceptions about the services offered. They may not fully understand the support available or fear that seeking assistance could be viewed negatively, such as assuming that it may negatively impact job application outcomes.
- **Fragmented Services**: VR services are provided by state agencies, and the availability and scope of services can vary from one state to another. This fragmentation can lead to inconsistent information and awareness about VR programs at the national level.
- **Complexity of the System**: The process of accessing VR services can sometimes be complex, involving multiple steps, disorganized websites, and extensive eligibility criteria. This complexity can deter some individuals from seeking assistance.
- **Competing Priorities**: For individuals with disabilities, navigating various support systems and government programs can be overwhelming. As a result, some may prioritize other forms of assistance or support over VR services.

- **Lack of Referrals**: Healthcare providers, schools, or other agencies that come in contact with individuals with disabilities may not always be aware of VR programs or may not consistently refer people to these services.
- **Limited Resources**: VR agencies may face budget constraints and limited staff, affecting their ability to conduct outreach and awareness campaigns effectively.
    - According to the **RSA Annual Report** for 2017-2020, the U.S. VR program had a federal appropriation of anywhere between $3.2 to $3.4 billion each year.

To address these challenges, it is crucial for VR agencies and advocacy groups to work together to increase public awareness about VR services. This can include targeted outreach efforts, educational materials, partnerships with community organizations, and improved communication with potential applicants and stakeholders.

Additionally, simplifying the application process (such as what has been done over the years to make the FAFSA easier to fill out) and improving coordination among various support systems can help make VR services more accessible and known to those who can benefit from them.

VR Services

VR services aim to assist individuals with disabilities in achieving their employment goals and increasing their independence. The specific services provided may vary depending on the individual's needs, a specific state's or country's VR program, and available resources.

Here is a list of common VR services —
- **Education and Training Tuition Assistance:** Financial assistance for eligible individuals to pursue education or training programs that enhance employability.
  - Training programs may include but are not limited to: community college, university, trade school, certification programs, apprenticeships, online courses, and more.
  - Related expenses they may cover include: purchasing interview clothing, application fees, paying for certain licenses, or exams that may be required within your field.
- **Assistive Technology**: Provision of tools, devices (such as needing a laptop for your work or studies), or software to help individuals with disabilities perform job tasks more efficiently.
- **Transportation Assistance:** Help with transportation to and from work, especially for individuals with mobility challenges.
- **Independent Living Services:** Support in areas such as housing, personal finance, and daily living skills to promote independent living.
- **Books and Supplies:** Some VR agencies may help cover the costs of required textbooks, course materials, and other essential supplies for your training.
- **Academic Support Services:** VR services may include academic support, tutoring, or counseling to help individuals with disabilities overcome any barriers to learning and successfully complete their college studies.
- **Job Training and Skills Development:** Training programs designed to enhance job-related skills and competencies in various industries.
- **Job Placement Assistance:** Assistance with job search, resume preparation, interview coaching, and connecting with employers.

- **Vocational Counseling**: Guidance and support from a VR counselor to explore career options, assess skills, and set employment goals.
- **Assessment and Evaluation**: Comprehensive evaluation of an individual's abilities, interests, and vocational potential to determine suitable career paths.
- **Workplace Accommodations**: Modifications to the work environment or job duties to accommodate specific disability-related needs.
- **Supported Employment:** Ongoing coaching for individuals with disabilities in the workplace to help them maintain employment.
- **On-the-Job Training:** Support for individuals to gain work experience and skills while being employed.
- **Transition Services**: Services designed to help students with disabilities transition from school to the workforce or further their education.
- **Vocational Rehabilitation Assessments:** Specific assessments to determine an individual's vocational aptitudes and interests.
- **Career Exploration Workshops:** Workshops to explore different career options and industries.
- **Entrepreneurship Support:** Assistance for individuals with disabilities who wish to start their own businesses.
- **Mental Health Support Services**: Counseling or therapy to address mental health challenges that may impact employment.
- **Job Retention Services:** Services to support individuals in maintaining their employment after job placement.
- **Community Resources Referral:** Providing information and connecting individuals with disabilities to community resources that can support their vocational goals.
- **Training in Self-Advocacy and Social Skills:** VR programs may provide training in self-advocacy, empowering individuals in recovery to express their needs and preferences confidently. Learning self-advocacy skills can be crucial in navigating educational settings, seeking employment opportunities, and accessing support services effectively.
- **Assistance with Medical Appointments and Treatment:** Some VR programs recognize the importance of ongoing medical treatment and support for individuals in recovery.

VR Eligibility

If you are accepted, VR can potentially continue to provide benefits even after you graduate from university, community college, trade school, etc.

Additionally, unlike many scholarships, VR doesn't require an essay. It doesn't have a deadline. Also, in many cases, it does not require a minimum GPA to maintain the benefits. However, if it does — as outlined in your "individualized plan" which we will discuss later in this book — that minimum might be around a 2.0 or 2.5 GPA to retain participation.

Eligibility criteria may vary slightly from state to state due to state-specific policies, but the core principles remain consistent.

Also, keep in mind that VR can be used by **working adults** with medical conditions as well. It is not limited to only incoming or current college students who are typically younger. So, if there is something you need specific training for that has a cost tied to it, or perhaps you need help with finding employment — **consider applying to VR as well!**

Here are the key eligibility requirements for VR services in the United States:
- **Disability Status:** The individual must have a disability that constitutes or results in a significant barrier to employment.
- **Functional Limitations:** The individual's condition must result in functional limitations that hinder their ability to perform certain work-related tasks or job duties. These limitations may affect physical abilities, cognitive functions, communication, or other essential job-related skills.
    - **TIP**: Be specific and articulate certain tasks within your desired career field that may be harder to do or impossible because of the symptoms of your condition.
    - For instance — individuals with respiratory disabilities may be sensitive to air quality and environmental factors, such as dust, allergens, smoke, and strong odors, which could impact their ability to work in certain settings.
- **Employment Impediment:** The condition must create a substantial impediment to obtaining or maintaining employment. This and "functional limitations" are perhaps the **MOST**

IMPORTANT parts of your application. There **NEEDS** to be a pre-existing OR anticipated correlation between your condition and how that has or will make it more difficult to secure a job, keep a job, or advance in your career due to the barriers it presents.

- ○ For instance, let's use vitiligo as an example which is according to the Oxford dictionary, "A condition in which the pigment is lost from areas of the skin, causing whitish patches, often with no clear cause." *The King of Pop famously had this condition*. A person who has vitiligo may find it harder in comparison to be hired and maintain a job due to implicit or conscious biases within society. Additionally, they would have difficulty getting a job that requires them to be out in the sun for long periods of time.
- ○ **TIP**: If you have not yet had any type of employment as it relates to your future career field, no worries! Instead, try to refer to research studies or personal accounts seen in news articles from those with your condition (who perhaps are already in the field you too want to pursue) who saw barriers to accessing employment due to their condition.

- **Age Requirement:** In most states, VR services are available to individuals with disabilities who are at least 16-years-old or older. Some states may have a minimum age requirement of 14 or 15 to receive certain pre-employment transition services for students with disabilities.
- **Employment Goal:** The applicant must have an employment goal and demonstrate their commitment to becoming employed, maintaining employment, or advancing in their career.
- **Citizenship or Residency**: Generally, VR services are available to — U.S. citizens, **OR** those from a U.S. territory **OR** individuals who are lawfully present in the United States.
  - ○ Some states may have additional residency requirements. So, check with your specific state's website and/or contact a VR counselor to confirm your eligibility.
- **Order of Selection (OOS):** In some states, there may be limited resources, and the VR agency may prioritize services for individuals with the most significant disabilities. This is known as

"Order of Selection," or OOS for short, and it means that individuals with the most severe disabilities receive services first.

- ○ As of 2023, there are 40 VR agencies that **are not** operating under an OOS.
- ○ And 38 VR agencies that **are** operating under an OOS.
- ○ To see if your state or U.S. territory prioritizes "more significant disabilities" or not, then refer to **this link** and scroll down to the graph below where it says "yes" or "no."

- **Suitability for VR Services:** The individual must demonstrate that they can benefit from VR services in terms of achieving their employment goals.
- **Cooperation and Participation:** The applicant must be willing to actively engage in the VR process and work collaboratively with the VR counselor to develop an Individualized Plan for Employment (IPE).
- **Financial need:** Some states may need to assess your financial need as part of the eligibility determination process. This assessment may involve the individual providing documentation of their income, assets, and other financial resources. This information helps the VR counselor understand the individual's financial need for vocational services and support.
  - ○ In the case of being a student, you will probably have to show your school's financial aid package offer, the school's cost of attendance per year, and any external aid you received (such as scholarships).
- **Disability Duration**: Some places may require a minimum of having the disability for 6 months, 12 months, or have no minimum at all.
  - ○ This varies depending on where you are, so make sure to consult with your local VR office for more information.
  - ○ Also, even if there is a minimum duration requirement, it doesn't mean that all disabilities must meet that specific criterion. VR counselors assess each individual's unique situation, including the nature and extent of the disability, its impact on their ability to work, and their vocational rehabilitation needs.

Additionally, you **do not** necessarily have to be enrolled full-time in higher education to receive VR services. In many cases, VR programs can support individuals who are enrolled **part-time** in education or vocational training programs. However, the specific requirements and provisions for VR services, including enrollment status, can vary depending on the policies of the VR program in your state or country. If you are enrolled full-time, you may expect to be required to take a minimum of 12 credit hours (four courses) per semester.

Finally, remember — **that being eligible does not guarantee immediate access to VR services.** Once determined eligible and accepted into the program, individuals may need to work with their VR counselor to develop an individualized plan, which outlines the specific services and support they will receive to achieve their employment goal. The VR agency will strive to provide services and support tailored to each individual's needs and circumstances to maximize their potential for successful employment outcomes.

WIOA Services

Under the Workforce Innovation and Opportunity Act (WIOA), eligible individuals may receive funding for a variety of workforce development and training expenses. The specific expenses covered by WIOA can vary based on the services offered by your local American Job Center or workforce development office. Generally, WIOA funding can cover the following expenses:

- **Tuition and Training Costs**: WIOA may cover the costs of tuition and fees for approved training programs, including vocational training, certificate programs, and postsecondary education (undergraduate, graduate school, etc).
- **Books and Supplies**: Funding may be available to help with the purchase of required textbooks, course materials, and supplies related to the approved training program.
- **Supportive Services**: WIOA may provide assistance with supportive services, such as transportation, childcare, and other necessary expenses to help participants overcome barriers to training and employment.
- **Occupational Tools and Equipment**: In certain cases, WIOA may cover the costs of tools, equipment, or uniforms required for specific occupations or industries.
- **Testing and Certification Fees:** Funding may be available to cover fees associated with required certifications or licensing exams related to the training program.
- **Job Search Assistance:** WIOA offers job search assistance, including resume writing, interview preparation, and job placement services.

Additionally, a wide range of courses and training programs may be covered, depending on the specific offerings and guidelines established by each state or local workforce development area. For instance —

- **Vocational Training Programs**: WIOA may cover vocational training programs that provide specific skills and knowledge for entry-level positions in various industries. Examples include healthcare assistant programs, information technology certifications, automotive technician training, and construction trades courses.

- **Certificate Programs:** WIOA funding can be used for short-term certificate programs that equip individuals with specialized skills for specific jobs or industries. Examples include paralegal certification, graphic design courses, culinary arts programs, and HVAC technician training.
- **Apprenticeship Programs**: WIOA supports apprenticeship programs that combine on-the-job training with classroom instruction. These programs are designed to prepare individuals for skilled trades and technical occupations.
- **Community College Courses**: Some WIOA programs may cover community college courses that lead to degrees, diplomas, or certifications. This includes associate degree programs and courses in various academic and technical fields.
- **Adult Education and Literacy Programs:** WIOA may support adult education and literacy programs that provide foundational skills, such as reading, writing, and math, to help individuals improve their employability.
- **English as a Second Language (ESL) Courses:** WIOA funding can be used for ESL courses to assist individuals with limited English proficiency in improving their language skills and accessing employment opportunities.
- **High-Demand Industries:** WIOA places a strong emphasis on training programs aligned with high-demand industries in the local labor market. These may include healthcare, information technology, advanced manufacturing, energy, and other growing sectors.

WIOA Eligibility + Funding

The eligibility criteria for the Workforce Innovation and Opportunity Act (WIOA) vary depending on the specific programs and services offered by each state and local workforce development area. However, there are general eligibility requirements that individuals must meet to be considered for WIOA services. Here are some common eligibility criteria.

- **Adults:** To be eligible as an adult under WIOA, you typically need to be at least 18 years old and either unemployed, underemployed, or facing a significant barrier to employment.
- **Youth:** WIOA provides services to eligible youth between the ages of 14 and 24. Eligibility criteria for youth can include factors such as economic need, basic skills deficiencies, and other barriers to employment or education.
- **Dislocated Workers:** Individuals who have been laid off or terminated from their jobs, are eligible for unemployment benefits, and are unlikely to return to their previous occupation due to various reasons like lack of demand, technological changes, or foreign competition, may be eligible as dislocated workers.
- **Low-Income Individuals:** WIOA often targets individuals from low-income households. Income eligibility criteria may vary depending on the local area and the specific program.
- **Individuals with Disabilities:** Individuals with disabilities, particularly those who face challenges in securing and maintaining employment due to their disabilities, are often eligible for WIOA services. Vocational rehabilitation services are also a part of WIOA.
- **Veterans:** Veterans and eligible spouses of veterans might receive priority for some WIOA programs and services.
- **Citizenship and Residency:** In most cases, individuals must be U.S. citizens or authorized to work in the United States. Residency requirements may also apply based on the specific program and the location of the services.

Also, keep in mind that local WIOA offices may have slightly different eligibility criteria and specific services based on the needs and resources of their respective regions.

The Disabled Debt-Free Degree

It is essential to **contact your local American Job Center** which may also be referred to as a "workforce development office" or "one-stop center" to inquire about specific eligibility requirements and available services in your area. They will be able to provide you with detailed information about eligibility and guide you through the application process. Eligibility determinations are made on a case-by-case basis, and WIOA programs aim to provide services to individuals who can benefit the most from employment and training assistance.

In terms of WIOA **financial assistance,** how much you receive can vary. For instance, according to **Med Certs**, if you qualify then textbooks, fees, and tuition will be covered up to $4,000. And according to **atlworks.org**, "You can receive up to $7,000 for a training that is up to one year and up to $10,000 for a training that is up to two years."

As seen on Med Certs website, funding also can include:
- A $25 stipend to spend on school supplies at the bookstore
- Funds for childcare of $15 a day for up to two children younger than 12 years old
- Gas money, depending on how far you must travel for class
- Reimbursement for some tests and supplies

Also, since I cited **MedCerts** here, I might as well mention some of the amazing work they're doing and how it may be of interest to you or perhaps someone you know. MedCerts is an online education and training provider that offers healthcare and IT certification programs. "MedCerts has partnered with American Job Centers as an approved training vendor in **30+ states.** You may be able to use the WIOA Grant to take their short-term training programs for national certifications in the healthcare and information technology (IT) industry" (MedCerts).

They offer a variety of self-paced, online courses and certification programs designed to prepare students for in-demand careers in fields such as medical coding and billing, pharmacy technician, medical office administration, medical assistant, IT support specialist, cybersecurity, and more. Feel free to check them out!

WIOA Funded Programs

Outside of funding VR, WIOA also funds a variety of programs and initiatives that are designed to provide employment and training services to individuals seeking to improve their skills and find gainful employment. Some examples of WIOA-funded programs include:

- **Workforce Training and Education Programs**: WIOA supports various training and education programs, including short-term training and certificate programs.
- **Adult Education and Literacy Programs:** WIOA supports adult education programs that provide basic education, English language instruction, and high school equivalency preparation (GED).
- **Youth Programs**: WIOA funds youth programs that offer educational and employment opportunities for young people.
- **Dislocated Worker Programs**: These programs assist individuals who have lost their jobs due to layoffs or economic disruptions (such as with obtaining unemployment insurance).
- **Apprenticeship Programs**: WIOA supports registered apprenticeship programs that provide on-the-job training and classroom instruction.
- **On-the-Job Training (OJT) Programs**: WIOA funds OJT initiatives where employers receive reimbursement for training new employees.
- **American Job Centers (AJCs)**: These centers offer a wide range of employment and training services, including job search assistance, career counseling, and skills development.
- **Supportive Services:** WIOA provides supportive services, such as transportation assistance and childcare, to help individuals overcome barriers to employment. Inquire about supportive services through your local AJC.

Please note that the availability of these programs may vary by state and local area. To access specific WIOA-funded programs, individuals should contact their local American Job Center or workforce development office for guidance and information tailored to their needs.

PART 2: The Application Phase - how to stand out with your application, interview hacks, and more

The Disabled Debt-Free Degree

By: Carlynn D. Greene

WIOA - How to Apply

This process may vary depending on where you reside, but here are some general pointers on how to apply for WIOA:

- **Find Your Local American Job Center (AJC):** The first step is to locate the nearest American Job Center in your area. AJCs are the primary access points for WIOA services. You can find your local AJC by visiting **careeronestop.org** and clicking on the "Find Local Help" tab seen at the top of the webpage. From there, type in your zip code (on the right side of the webpage) and once you press "search" you will see a list of Workforce Solution Centers near you.
- **Contact the AJC:** Once you identify the local AJC, reach out to them by phone or visit in person. You can inquire about the services available, eligibility criteria, and the application process for WIOA programs.
- **Meet with a Career Counselor or Case Manager:** The AJC will likely schedule an appointment for you to meet with a career counselor or case manager. During this meeting, they will assess your needs, career goals, and eligibility for WIOA programs.
- **Provide Documentation**: You may be required to provide certain documents to support your eligibility for WIOA services. These documents may include a state identification card, proof of citizenship or legal residency, income verification, and documentation related to your employment and educational history.
- **Determine Eligibility**: Based on the assessment, the AJC will then determine if you meet the eligibility criteria for WIOA services and which specific programs you may qualify for.
- **Develop an Individual Employment Plan (IEP)**: If you are deemed eligible for WIOA services, you will work with your career counselor or case manager to develop an Individual Employment Plan (IEP). The IEP outlines your employment goals, the services you will receive, and the steps you need to take to achieve your objectives.
- **Access WIOA Services**: Once your IEP is in place, you can start accessing WIOA services. These services may include job search assistance, career counseling, skills training, and more.

VR Paperwork Needed Checklist

When applying for Vocational Rehabilitation (VR) services, you may need to complete paperwork to initiate the process. Here's a general checklist of common documents you might need.

- **Application Form**: Fill out the VR agency's application form. The form requires personal information, contact details, and a brief description of your disability and vocational goals.
- **Proof of Disability**: Provide medical or psychological documentation that verifies your disability and its impact on your ability to work. This may include doctor's reports, medical records, or evaluations.
- **Photo Proof of Identity**: Provide a valid form of identification such as a driver's license, state ID, school ID, or passport.
    - If you don't have these, you can still apply for services.
    - However, you must verify that you can legally work in the United States by providing work authorization documents or a Social Security number.
- **Proof of Residency or Citizenship**: Provide documentation to verify your residency or citizenship status, such as a utility bill, lease agreement, or birth certificate.
- **Tax Information**: If you were employed, submit your and your parents' most recent tax returns.
- **Social Security Number (SSN)**: Provide your SSN for identification and eligibility verification purposes. They may also need a copy of the physical SSN card, so have that readily available just in case.
- **Insurance Information**: In some cases, they may need a picture of your insurance card on the front and back.
- **Education Records**: Submit official transcripts or records of your educational history. This includes a high school diploma, college degrees, and vocational training certificates.
    - **NOTE**: Official transcripts are different from unofficial transcripts. Unofficial ones are typically free from your institution. However, official ones may have a small fee.
- **Work History:** Provide details of your work history, including past employers, job titles, and dates of employment.
- **Resume**: Prepare a current resume that highlights your skills, qualifications, and work experiences.

- **Financial Information**: Some VR agencies may require information about your financial status including income, assets, and household size.
- **Individualized Plan for Employment (IPE)**: If you have already started the VR process and developed an IPE with your VR counselor, bring a copy of the plan or any related documents.
- **Proof of Income or Expenses**: While not commonly needed, some agencies may require your mortgage or rent bill.
- **Recurring Medical Expenses**: Needed in some cases, such as for prescription drugs.
- **Other Supporting Documents**: Depending on your specific circumstances and vocational goals, you may need to provide letters of recommendation, certifications, or licenses.

As a tip — try to have all this documentation organized in both a **password-protected digital folder** and **physically printed out** in a folder or binder. If possible, bring as many documents as possible to your first meeting with a VR counselor to speed up the evaluation process.

To ensure you have all the necessary documents for your application, contact your local VR agency directly and look on their website for the needed information.

Letter from Your Doctor

VR typically requires comprehensive information about the individual's disability or medical condition. The documentation should come from a qualified healthcare professional like a licensed physician, psychiatrist, psychologist, or other specialist.

- **Diagnosis**: The medical documentation should include a clear and specific diagnosis of the disability or medical condition. The diagnosis should be based on a thorough evaluation of the individual's medical history, symptoms, and any relevant medical tests or assessments.
- **Medical History**: The healthcare professional should provide a summary of the individual's medical history related to the disability. They will document the onset of symptoms, progression of the condition, how long the person had this condition, and any previous treatments or interventions.
- **Functional Limitations**: The medical documentation should outline the functional limitations caused by the disability. This includes how the condition affects the individual's ability to work, learn in school, and daily living activities.
- **Impact on Employment**: The healthcare professional may need to explain how the disability impacts the person's employment opportunities. This information **is crucial** for VR counselors to determine eligibility and appropriate vocational services.
- **Treatment and Medication**: Details about current and past treatments, medications, and therapies. Any assistive devices or accommodations used by the individual should be included.
- **Prognosis**: If applicable, the medical documentation may include the expected prognosis or course of the disability over time.
- **Signatures and Credentials**: The medical documentation should be signed by a qualified healthcare professional and should include their credentials, contact information, and the date of evaluation. In some cases, having your school's 504 coordinator's signature as well might help.

Also, the medical documentation might have to be very **recent, like within a year**. The documentation should be written in a clear and detailed manner, providing a comprehensive understanding of the individual's disability and its impact on their ability to work.

So, provide your doctor with the information shared in this chapter to help them with outlining and writing their letter. Communicating directly with them can increase your chances of qualifying for the VR program.

There should be an **emphasis** on how your condition can potentially (or has already) **impede your ability to work.**

Later on, in the chapter titled **Templates / Scripts to Use**, you will find a **template** on how to reach out to a medical professional to write this letter for you.

Process for Tribal / Native Nations

For Native Americans belonging to tribal nations, accessing VR services in the United States can be a bit different because of the available tribal vocational rehabilitation programs. These programs operate in conjunction with state VR agencies to provide specialized services tailored to the unique needs and cultural backgrounds of Native American individuals with disabilities.

Each federally recognized tribal nation may have its own VR program that operates under the authority of the Rehabilitation Act and the Indian Self-Determination and Education Assistance Act. These programs receive funding from the U.S. Department of Education's Rehabilitation Services Administration (RSA) and work to deliver VR services to eligible Native Americans with disabilities.

To find a Tribal Nation VR Center, use **this link** and search for your specific state. About half of U.S. states are listed here. Also please note that this resource link was published as of September 2020, so some of the contact information might be a bit dated. If the contacts listed end up not working (*such as the person mentioned no longer working at that VR center)*, then instead:

- Paste in the physical address of a center in your state into Google and find their up-to-date contact information from there.
- Or type on Google the name of your tribe(s) x your state and "vocational rehabilitation"

Additionally, consider looking into the **Assistance for Indian Children with Severe Disabilities** — a program that provides special education and related services. To contact them, call the number on **this page.**

VR & WIOA Locator

Here is a **full list** of vocational rehabilitation agencies with their contact information that are based in the U.S. and territories.

There are **78 VR agencies**:

- **22** states have each established two VR agencies (making a total of 44): one VR agency that serves individuals who are blind or have visual impairments, referred to as **Blind VR agencies** — and a separate VR agency that serves individuals with all other types of disabilities, referred to as **General VR agencies**.
- **34** states and territories have one VR agency that serves individuals with all types of disabilities (including for the blind); these are referred to as **Combined VR agencies.**

Instead of first contacting your state's overall VR agency seen from the link above you can **contact your LOCAL center** that is nearest to you to schedule an appointment with a counselor to potentially get a faster response.

This process can be somewhat confusing to do on your own. Many state VR agencies and local VR offices have **different names.** For instance, they may be referred to as — the Department of Rehabilitation Services, Department of Human Services, Department of Workforce Development, and so forth. Also, some VR locators or directories aren't easily found on the state's website.

How very accessible, right?

Just yet another example of why I needed to write this book.

With that being said, I went ahead and did the work for you! In this **Google spreadsheet**, you will find all these direct links to each state's VR locator. From there, a state or territory may ask for your zip code or county to find a VR office nearest to you. Here's how to use the spreadsheet:

- **Instructions:** Make sure that you are **signed into a Google account** and press the blue button that says, **"make a copy."** Then from there, you can customize it as needed.

- On the spreadsheet's **second tab**, you will find direct links to VR offices that are specifically for the **blind / visually impaired.**
- If a URL link seen on the spreadsheet needs updating (since these may be prone to changing over time) simply email me. You can find my contact information at the end of this book.

Additionally, within the spreadsheet, you will find direct links to local **WIOA-eligible training programs** based in your state or territory (including Guam and the U.S. Virgin Islands, but not Puerto Rico or American Samoa).

I suggest first **calling** and then emailing before visiting their offices. Some VR offices may be understaffed, so to ensure that you are going to get the help you need, contact the office prior to your visit.

Finally, make sure that you are reaching out to a vocational rehabilitation services center and **NOT** a rehabilitation center (meaning, those recovering from certain conditions). There's a difference!

Templates / Scripts to Use

When you call VR or WIOA make sure to mention that you are inquiring about their **"education and training services."** Here is a possible condensed script —

- **Script for VR:** "Hello! My name is ____. I would like to speak with a counselor to determine my eligibility for the vocational rehabilitation program relating to education and training services."
- **Script for WIOA:** "Hello! My name is ____. I would like to speak with a case manager to determine my eligibility for WIOA relating to education and training services."

Here are some more detailed templates / scripts to use in other scenarios relating to VR or WIOA. Feel free to either use this in an email or verbally over the phone. Customize as needed when you are sending this out.

- **Template scripts linked here**
- **Instructions:** Make sure that you are **signed into a Google account** and press the blue button that says, **"Make a copy"**
- From there customize as needed

In this Google document, you will find the following **templates / scripts:**

- Inquiring About VR Services
- Request Needing Documentation from Medical Professional
- VR Application Denied
- VR Says Your Request is "Too Expensive"
- VR Doesn't Believe Your Disability Affects Employment
- VR Denied Due to Already Having a Degree

Getting No Response?

If you are experiencing a lack of response from a VR or WIOA office, it can be frustrating and concerning. However, there are several steps you can take to address the situation and ensure that your needs are met:

- **Follow Up**: Consider following up with them multiple times. Communication delays can happen, and a gentle reminder may prompt them to get back to you.
- **Contact Multiple Channels**: Try reaching out to the agency through different channels such as phone, email, or in-person if possible. This approach increases the chances of getting a response, as some agencies may be more responsive through other methods.
- **Explore Alternative Offices**: Depending on your location, there may be multiple offices that serve different regions within your area. If you are facing challenges with one agency, you can reach out to another agency that can assist you. Keep in mind that offices in more populated cities may receive more inquiries in comparison to less populated areas. This may also be a strategy to consider using to get a faster response.
- **Be Persistent and Patient**: Certain offices may be dealing with a high volume of cases or staff shortages which can lead to delays in responses. While being persistent, also be patient and give them some time to get back to you.
- **Contact Higher Authorities**: If the lack of response persists, you can consider contacting higher authorities. For VR, you can find the state-level contact info **here**. They can help escalate your case and ensure that your inquiry receives attention.
- **Attend In-Person or Virtual Events**: Some VR agencies host workshops, open houses, or virtual events. You can meet with VR counselors and ask questions about the services available. Attending such events may facilitate direct communication with agency representatives.
- **Reach Out to Your Counselor's Supervisor**: If you have been assigned a VR counselor and are having difficulty getting in touch with them, consider contacting their supervisor to express your concerns.

- **Seek Help from Advocacy Organizations**: If you are experiencing difficulties with the VR agency, reach out to disability advocacy organizations in your area. They may be able to offer guidance, support, or even intervene on your behalf.
- **Keep Records**: Throughout your interactions with the VR agency keep a record of the dates and methods of communication. For example, any emails or phone calls sent or received should be documented. This documentation can be helpful if you need to escalate your concerns.

Remember that VR agencies are there to assist individuals with disabilities, and their mission is to provide support and services to help you reach your vocational goals.

If you encounter challenges in getting a response, **advocate for yourself** and seek assistance from other resources.

The Unofficial Interview

During the first meeting with a VR counselor or WIOA case manager, the focus is usually on gathering information about the individual's disability, vocational goals, and needs. Although it is not a formal interview, you should think of it that way.

During the meeting, they determine whether or not you are suitable for the program. The meeting can last anywhere from a couple of minutes to an hour.

Some questions that a **VR counselor** may potentially ask during the first meeting include:
- What is your disability or medical condition? Please define it.
- What is your current employment status and work history?
- What type of job or career are you interested in pursuing?
    - **TIP**: If your motivation to pursue a certain career path relates to your disability then mention that! For instance — If you have X medical condition and as a result want to be an accident injury lawyer, a certain type of nurse, etc.
- Have you received any previous vocational or employment services or training?
- Are there any specific challenges or barriers you face in achieving your vocational goals as they relate to your disabilities? What specific symptoms?
    - This is arguably the **MOST** important question. Try to envision yourself already working at your desired job. Then from there, think of scenarios in which your job performance may be impacted by your medical condition.
- What types of accommodations or support services do you believe you may need in the workplace?
    - If asked this, make sure to review over the services covered earlier in this book for VR.

Some questions that a **WIOA case manager** may potentially ask during the first meeting include:
- What are your career goals and aspirations?
- What type of job or industry are you interested in pursuing?
- Do you have a specific training program or course in mind?

- Have you been actively looking for a job?
- What skills and qualifications do you possess that are relevant to your career goals?
- Are there any specific job search or skill development needs you have?
- Are you currently employed? If so, what is your current job?
- Are you receiving any government assistance or benefits (e.g., SNAP, TANF, unemployment)?
- Do you have any financial barriers to employment or training?

Some may experience a second meeting before eligibility can be determined. The questions asked in subsequent meetings will likely be more focused on progress updates and reassessing goals. The counselor's questions are designed to understand the individual's needs, and aspirations to help them achieve meaningful and sustainable employment outcomes.

Practice makes perfect! Take the time to do a **mock interview** with a parent, friend, school counselor, or classmate. Try answering these questions over and over again until you feel comfortable with how you respond. It is important to listen to the feedback and feel confident.

You also **might be allowed to have a parent or another person accompany you.** Depending on your medical condition it may be mandatory. For instance, if you need someone to interpret sign language, or perhaps you have Tourette's or other communication conditions, someone can help with articulating your background and requests. In that case, the person assisting you should also have a strong understanding of how to answer the questions seen above in this chapter.

Finally, try to dress in business casual clothing, arrive early, and make sure to ask questions. Towards the end ask about when you can expect to hear back from them with updates and results.

More Interview Strategies

Here are some tips to help you make the most of your conversation.

- **Prepare for the Meeting**: Take some time to gather your thoughts and any relevant documents before the meeting. If you have a resume, educational records, or medical documentation related to your disability (if applicable) bring them along. Being organized will help you present your case clearly.
- **Clarify Your Goals**: Think about what you want to achieve. Identify your career interests, strengths, and areas where you need support. Having a clear idea of your goals will allow the counselor to better assist you in creating a plan.
- **Be Open and Honest**: The counselor is there to help you, so don't hesitate to share your concerns, challenges, and aspirations openly. The more information you provide, the better the counselor can tailor their assistance to your specific needs.
- **Ask Questions**: Don't be afraid to ask questions during the meeting. Seek clarification on any aspect of the vocational rehabilitation process that you're uncertain about.
- **Listen and Take Notes**: Pay close attention to the counselor's guidance and recommendations. Take notes during the meeting, so you have a reference to review later. This will help you remember important details and action steps discussed.
- **Advocate for Yourself**: Remember, you are an active participant in the process. If there's something you feel strongly about or if you believe certain services or accommodations would be beneficial for you, express your thoughts to the counselor.
- **Discuss Challenges and Barriers**: Be open about any challenges you face that may impact your employment prospects.
- **Explore Opportunities**: Engage in a conversation about potential career options and training programs that align with your interests and abilities. The counselor may provide valuable insights into industries and opportunities you haven't considered.
- **Follow Up**: After the meeting, if there are action items or steps to take, follow up promptly. Take the necessary actions to move your vocational plan forward, and stay in touch with the counselor regularly to provide updates.

The Psych Test

A psychological evaluation is sometimes conducted to assess an individual's mental health, cognitive abilities, emotional functioning, and other psychological factors that may impact their ability to work and participate in vocational activities. The evaluation helps the VR counselor gain a comprehensive understanding of the individual's strengths, challenges, and needs. This is essential when developing an effective Individualized Plan for Employment (IPE) tailored to the person's specific requirements.

If you are requested to undergo a psychological evaluation, it's crucial to be open and honest during the assessment to ensure the most accurate information is obtained. The evaluation is intended to support you in achieving your vocational goals and enhancing your overall well-being.

Here are some reasons why a psychological evaluation might be included in the VR process —

- **Disability Assessment**: The evaluation can help identify the presence of psychological or cognitive disabilities that may be affecting the individual's ability to work or access employment opportunities.
- **Functional Limitations**: It helps determine the extent to which the psychological condition may impact the individual's daily functioning, including work-related tasks.
- **Accurate Vocational Planning**: Understanding the individual's psychological profile allows the VR counselor to develop a realistic and achievable vocational plan that aligns with the person's abilities and needs.
- **Identifying Support Needs:** The evaluation may reveal the need for specific accommodations or support services that can enhance the individual's vocational success.
- **Treatment and Interventions**: If mental health issues are identified, the evaluation can help guide appropriate treatment and interventions that may improve the individual's ability to engage in vocational activities.
- **Employment Considerations**: The evaluation may assist in identifying suitable employment options based on the individual's psychological strengths and limitations.

If you are asked to do a psych test, make sure to **prep beforehand.** For instance, you might be expected to answer questions relating to **qualities needed within the career field you want.**

For example, if someone is considering a career in a **technical field**, the psychological evaluation may include tests that assess their mechanical aptitude, problem-solving abilities, and spatial reasoning.

On the other hand, if someone is interested in a career in **counseling or communication**, the evaluation might include tests to assess their interpersonal skills, empathy, and communication style.

Finally, it's important to note that a psychological evaluation is conducted by a qualified psychologist or mental health professional. The process is confidential, and the results are used solely for the purpose of assisting the individual in their vocational rehabilitation journey.

For Out-of-State Students

The availability of VR services for out-of-state students may vary depending on a specific state's policies and regulations. Vocational rehabilitation services are typically provided by state agencies, and each state has its own guidelines and eligibility criteria.

If you are an out-of-state student seeking VR services, the **best course of action** is to first contact a local VR office **in the state you're originally from.**

Then **if that doesn't work** out and your application is rejected, then contact a local VR office in the state where you are currently studying.

In many cases, VR services are primarily designed to assist individuals with disabilities who are residents of the state. However, some states may have provisions or agreements that allow out-of-state students to access these services if they meet certain requirements. Some states may require you to live there for an entire year to earn resident status (this duration varies from state to state).

Here is a helpful **article** covering several ways on how to **establish residency** in a state and the **tuition benefits** of doing so.

Also, keep in mind that funding for an out-of-state college can be more challenging to obtain compared to in-state education. If you are still in the process of applying to colleges out-of-state you might have to **really advocate for yourself** and demonstrate that attending an out-of-state institution is necessary to achieve your vocational goals and that the specific services or programs you need are not available in your state.

For instance, let's say that you want to become a veterinarian. However, you live outside of one of the **20+ states** in the U.S. that has an accredited veterinary school. Therefore, you need to study out-of-state in order to pursue your vocational goals.

For Graduate / Ph.D. Students

In the United States, the VR program can potentially be used to support individuals with disabilities pursuing graduate studies, law school, medical school, nursing school, and other advanced degree programs. There have been many students in advanced degree programs who qualified for the program and secured funding for their education.

Here are some examples:
- **Law school** *(via the National Disabled Law Student Association)*
- **Medical school** *(via Reddit, specifically VR&E)*

Keep in mind that funding is **not guaranteed.** Certain types of master's or doctoral programs may receive more funding than others. Also, there may be a priority to fund undergraduate studies. With that being said, you will have to **really make a case for yourself** to prove that you are capable of pursuing that degree.

It may help to share with your VR counselor your admissions letter, academic honors, and recommendation letters from professors.

Denied or Waitlisted

If your VR or WIOA application is rejected or waitlisted, there are steps you can take to address the situation.

Here are some recommended actions —

- **Request an Explanation for Rejection**: If your application is rejected, request a written explanation from the counselor or case manager detailing the reasons for the decision. Understanding the specific reasons for the rejection can help you identify any potential issues that need to be addressed.
- **Appealing Process**: This stands for "Client Assistance Program," and it is a federally funded program designed to provide assistance and advocacy services to individuals with disabilities who are seeking or receiving services from VR. If you have been rejected (such as if you believe the rejection was unfair or unjustified), CAP can guide you through the **appeals process** and help you file complaints if needed.
    - For **VR**, contact your state's CAP office directly via phone or email. To find their contact info, simply type in on Google: **[Your state's name] x Client Assistance Program.**
    - However, some CAP offices for certain states may be harder to locate. If that is the case then — request assistance with your specific vocational rehabilitation concerns or questions, and they can guide you through the process and provide support.
    - For **WIOA**, if denied, contact your local American Job Center (AJC) or workforce development agency.
- **Appeal on Your Own**: If you believe that your application was unfairly rejected or that there was a misunderstanding, you have the right to appeal the decision. Contact the counselor / case manager or overall local office for VR or WIOA to learn about the appeal process and deadlines. Be prepared to provide any relevant evidence or documentation that supports your appeal.
- **Inquire About the Waitlist**: Contact the VR or WIOA in your state to inquire about the waitlist status and estimated wait times. Understanding the timeframe can help you plan accordingly.

- **Review Eligibility Criteria**: Review the eligibility to ensure that you meet all the requirements. If there are any discrepancies or missing documentation, consider providing additional information to support your eligibility.
- **Explore Other Options**: If you are waitlisted or unable to access, consider exploring other assistance programs in your area. State community-based organizations may offer similar services.
- **Stay Informed**: Stay informed about updates or changes to the VR or WIOA programs policies and eligibility criteria. Reapply if your circumstances change or if you believe you meet the eligibility requirements in the future.
- **Apply in a Different State**: If you are, let's say, an out-of-state student, it might be worth it to apply in the other state you are associated with. Again, it is recommended to apply in the state you are originally based in. However, if that ends up not working out, apply in the state you now reside in.
- **Seek Guidance from Veterans Service Organizations**: If a veteran specifically, **Veterans Service Organizations** (**VSOs**) can offer valuable assistance and guidance in navigating the VR&E application process and potential appeals. They have experience working with veterans and understanding the programs and benefits available to them.

As is with any type of application — patience, persistence, and seeking support from relevant resources can be key to navigating the process and accessing the services you need.

Reapplying Strategy

When reapplying to VR, it's essential to approach the process thoughtfully and strategically.

Here are some steps and tips, including how to improve your interview with the counselor —

- **Assess Your Situation**: Take time to evaluate any changes in your disability or employment status that may impact your eligibility for VR services. Understanding your current needs and goals will help you make a stronger case during the reapplication.
- **Gather Updated Documentation**: Ensure you have up-to-date and relevant documentation that supports your disability and its impact on your ability to work or pursue education. This may include medical records, evaluations, and any other relevant reports.
- **Review Previous Application**: Reflect on your previous application to identify areas where you can improve. Consider whether there were any missing documents or information that could strengthen your case this time.
- **Contact a Different VR Office**: By going to a different local office and meeting with a different VR counselor, you might see different results.
- **Request a Meeting**: Reach out to your local VR office and schedule a meeting with a counselor. Use this opportunity to discuss your situation, explain any changes, and demonstrate your commitment to your vocational goals.
- **Emphasize Your Goals**: Clearly articulate your career or education aspirations and how VR services can assist you in achieving them. Show your determination and motivation to succeed with the support of VR.
- **Address Previous Concerns**: If your previous application was not accepted, address any concerns raised during that process. Be prepared to discuss how you have addressed or overcome those issues.
- **Seek Feedback**: If possible, ask for feedback from your previous interview to gain insights on areas you can improve. Use this feedback to refine your approach and be better prepared for the new interview.

- **Enhance Your Interview Skills**: Practice answering interview questions with a focus on effectively communicating your abilities, goals, and how VR can be instrumental in your success. If you previously did not have someone with you during your meeting with a VR counselor, try to do so this time around and have them advocate for you.
- **Stay Persistent**: The application process can take time, so be patient and persistent. Follow up with the VR office if you don't hear back within a reasonable timeframe.
- **Seek Additional Support**: Consider seeking assistance from a disability advocate or support organization to help you navigate the reapplication process and provide guidance.

VR & WIOA Timeline Summary

I know that this was a lot of information all at once, so I wanted to also provide you with a summary timeline on what the process may look like from A to Z.

1. **Initial Contact:** Reach out to your local VR or WIOA office to express your interest in the program. You can do this by phone, email, or by visiting the office in person. Preferably do so via phone and inquire about "training services" for education.
   a. Try to do so **three to four months** before the start of the semester / training so that if accepted, the funds are more likely to come just in time when your tuition bill is due.
2. **Application**: Complete the VR or WIOA application form and provide any required documentation, such as proof of disability, medical records, and identification. Submit the application to the VR or WIOA office.
3. **Assessment:** Once your application is received, you may be scheduled for an initial assessment or interview with a VR counselor or WIOA case manager. During this meeting, you will discuss your disability, vocational goals, and any barriers to employment.
   a. Make sure to have your paperwork folder or binder with you to speed up the process!
4. **Eligibility Determination**: The VR or WIOA counselor will review your application and assessment to determine if you meet the eligibility criteria for VR or WIOA services.
   a. This usually happens about **two months after** the application's submission date.
5. **Individualized Plan**: Together with your VR or WIOA counselor, you will develop an individualized plan that outlines your vocational goals, and the services and supports you need to achieve those goals. It may also include any necessary training or education.
   a. This process typically happens **within three months** from eligibility.
6. **Plan Implementation**: Once the plan is approved, the VR or WIOA services outlined in the plan will be provided to help you

reach your employment objectives. This may include job training, counseling, placement assistance, and other support services.

7. **Progress Monitoring:** Throughout the process, your VR or WIOA counselor will regularly review your progress and make any necessary adjustments to the plan.

8. **Employment:** The ultimate goal of VR or WIOA is to help you secure meaningful employment that aligns with your abilities and goals. Once you are employed, VR or WIOA may continue to provide ongoing support and follow-up services as needed.

PART 3: The Inducted Stage - once accepted, what to expect in the beginning and throughout

The Disabled Debt-Free Degree

By: Carlynn D. Greene

You're Accepted, But Now What?

Congratulations on qualifying for VR or WIOA services! The next steps involve working closely with your VR counselor or WIOA case manager to develop an **individualized plan** tailored to your specific vocational goals and needs. Here's what you can potentially expect to experience:

- **Assessment Summary**: The plan may include a summary of the vocational assessment conducted by the counselor or case manager. This summary highlights the individual's strengths, skills, interests, barriers, and vocational rehabilitation needs.
- **Services and Supports**: The plan outlines the specific services and support that will be provided to the individual. This may include vocational training, education, job placement assistance, assistive technology, job coaching, transportation assistance, and other resources as needed.
- **Timeline and Duration**: The plan may include a timeline that outlines the expected duration of each service and the overall plan. It provides a roadmap for the individual's vocational journey.
- **Accommodations and Assistive Technology**: If applicable, the plan includes any necessary workplace accommodations and assistive technology that will be provided to support the individual's employment success.
- **Career Counseling and Guidance**: The plan may detail the career counseling and guidance services that the individual will receive throughout their vocational journey.
- **Supportive Services**: Supportive services, such as childcare assistance or transportation support, may be included if they are essential to the individual's participation in services.
- **Employment Plan**: The plan may include a step-by-step employment plan that outlines the specific actions the individual will take to achieve their vocational goal.
- **Academic or Training Requirements**: If the individual is participating in vocational training or education, the plan may specify the academic performance standards or training requirements they need to meet to continue receiving VR support.
- **Participation in Services**: The individual is generally expected to actively participate in the agreed-upon services and follow

through with the recommended actions to work towards their vocational goal.

- **Meet with Your VR Counselor**: Your VR counselor will be your main point of contact throughout the process. Schedule an appointment with them to discuss your eligibility, share information about your disability, and outline your vocational aspirations.
    - ○ **NOTE**: If for whatever reason, you cannot make a scheduled meeting — do not panic! Simply let them know in advance so you can reschedule.
- **Review and Approval**: Once the plan is developed, you will have the opportunity to review and approve it. Make sure you understand all the services and goals outlined in the plan before giving your consent.
- **Implementation:** Once the plan is approved, your counselor will start implementing the plan. This may involve enrolling you in training programs, connecting you with potential employers, or providing other services as outlined in the plan.
- **Continuous Communication**: Stay in regular communication with your VR counselor. Update them on your progress, discuss any challenges, and inform them of any circumstance changes.
- **Work Towards Employment Goals**: Take an active role in working towards your employment goals. Participate in training, attend job interviews, and put your best effort into the process.
- **Regular Assessments**: Periodic assessments will be conducted to evaluate your progress and make any necessary adjustments to the plan. This may be quarterly, bi-annually, once a year, or just as needed (such as where there are significant changes in the individual's circumstances, employment status, or vocational goals).
- **Successful Employment**: The ultimate goal of VR or WIOA services is to help you achieve successful employment and gain independence in your chosen career path.

Finally, make sure to **take full advantage** of the resources and opportunities provided to achieve your vocational goals!

Remember Your Plan

I understand life can get hectic and it can be very easy to forget your individualized plan. However, it is **crucial** to stay on track to **avoid disqualification** of VR or WIOA services.

Yes, some people have experienced this, so don't let it happen to you!

With that being said, here are some tips to help you remember and adhere to your plan:

- **Keep a Physical Copy**: Obtain a printed copy of your plan, and keep it in a safe and accessible place. Review it regularly to refresh your memory about the specific goals, services, and requirements outlined in the plan.
- **Create a Checklist**: Create a summarized version of your plan with checkoff boxes to mark off completed tasks. Create a timeline on when you should have that certain goal done by. If you are a visual person, put that somewhere you can see it every day.
- **Digital Reminders**: Create digital reminders on your smartphone or computer to review your plan regularly. It may be useful to set up calendar events or alarms to check your progress and any upcoming milestones.
- **Visual Aids**: Create visual aids or infographics summarizing your plan's key points (perhaps in vision board format). Hang these in a visible place, such as on your refrigerator or workspace.
- **Set Specific Goals**: Break down the goals in your plan into smaller achievable tasks with specific timelines. This way, you can track your progress more effectively and stay motivated.
- **Use Note-taking Apps**: Utilize note-taking apps or productivity tools to jot down important details from your individualized plan. You can refer back to these notes whenever needed.
- **Regular Check-ins with VR Counselor**: Schedule regular check-in meetings with your VR counselor to discuss your progress and any challenges you may be facing. These meetings will help keep you accountable and ensure you are on track.
- **Involve a Support Network**: Share your vocational goals and plan details with trusted family members, friends, or mentors.

The Best Assigned Person for YOU

Similar to any type of counselor (such as school counselors or mental health counselors), your experience may be drastically different depending on **who** exactly you are assigned.

That is why it is important to get the right VR counselor or WIOA case manager for YOU. Here are some steps you can take to ensure you work with an experienced counselor:

- **Ask for Recommendations**: Seek recommendations from other individuals who have gone through the process.
- **Inquire About Experience**: When contacting the VR agency, ask about the experience level of the available counselors. Request to work with a counselor who has experience working with individuals with similar disabilities or vocational goals as yours.
- **Research Profiles**: Some offices may provide counselor or case manager profiles on their websites, so check their bios.
- **Request a Consultation**: Request a consultation or initial meeting with a counselor to discuss your vocational goals, needs, and concerns. This will allow you to get a sense of their experience and approach to counseling.
- **Ask About Specializations**: Inquire if the VR agency has counselors who specialize in certain areas such as working with specific disability types, particular career industries, or have experience with helping people fund their higher education.
- **Advocate for Your Needs**: If you feel that your assigned person may not have the experience or expertise you need, don't hesitate to advocate for yourself. Politely express your preferences and discuss the importance of working with a counselor who can best support your vocational goals.
- **Review Agency Policies**: Some VR agencies may allow you to request a change of counselor if the initial match is not suitable. Check with the agency about their policies regarding counselor assignments.
- **Seek Feedback**: If you are working with a counselor and feel that the support provided is not meeting your expectations, provide feedback to the counselor or the agency to hopefully improve your experience.

Getting Reimbursement

In some cases, VR programs may be able to reimburse individuals for certain education-related expenses that a student has already paid. However, the specific rules and policies regarding reimbursement can vary depending on the state and the VR program's guidelines.

Here are some important points to consider —

- **Eligibility for Reimbursement:** Expect specific criteria for reimbursement eligibility. Typically, the expenses must be related to an approved service or accommodation outlined in an individualized plan.
- **Pre-Approval**: It is essential to get pre-approval from your VR counselor before making any payments or incurring expenses. In some cases, VR programs may not reimburse expenses that were not previously approved in your IPE. So **always ASK** first before making a purchase.
- **Receipts and Documentation**: To seek reimbursement, you will need to provide documentation and receipts.
- **Timing of Reimbursement**: It may take some time for VR or WIOA to process and approve reimbursement requests. It's essential to discuss the process and timeline with your counselor or case manager.
- **Expense Types**: There may be specific guidelines on the types of expenses that can be reimbursed. For example:
  - tuition, fees, books, supplies, and other education-related costs
- **Reimbursement Limitations**: Some VR programs may have limitations on the amount of reimbursement they can provide for certain expenses. So be sure to clarify any limits beforehand.

On the other hand, let's say that you are taking courses that either VR or WIOA is funding — but then decide to drop a course and receive a refund check from your school. Or you already received funding to complete a certain test or certification, but then later on decided not to move forward with doing that.

With these scenarios — do you keep that money, or do you reimburse it?

Well, some VR or WIOA offices may require you to return the money to them, while others may allow you to keep the refund but adjust the funding they provide you with for future expenses accordingly.

To ensure compliance with your VR or WIOA program's rules, promptly inform your counselor or case manager about the course drop (or any other academic scenario) and the refund you received. They will guide you on the appropriate steps to take, whether that involves returning the refund to VR or making adjustments to your funding for future educational expenses.

Partial vs. Full Funding

We have already established that for WIOA specifically, the **funding cap** for training may be around **$4,000-$10,000** depending on your program, where you are, and so forth. However, for VR, keep in mind that not every student will receive a full financial package, but might instead receive partial aid. In that case, here are some options to look into.

- **Negotiate with the VR Counselor:** Talk to your VR counselor about the possibility of securing additional funding or accommodations. They may be able to advocate on your behalf or explore other funding options within the VR program.
- **Testing Out of College Credits:** If you are a student receiving partial funding, consider using part of your funds for CLEP or AP exams (*have this outlined in your individualized plan).*
  - **Fun Fact**: In some cases, even adults can still take AP exams. However, you will have to find a high school or local testing center that is willing to seat you for the exam.
  - The CLEP exam is very similar to AP in that you can test out for college credits and potentially save a lot of money. To search which schools accept CLEP credits, click **here**.
  - To learn more about this process, refer to this **document** I put together.
- **Community Resources:** Research local community foundations, organizations, and nonprofits, that provide financial assistance for individuals with disabilities pursuing education or vocational training.
- **Explore Alternative Funding Sources:** Look into other financial aid options, scholarships, grants, or tuition assistance programs that may help cover the remaining expenses. Many educational institutions offer financial aid packages and scholarships for students. There may be specific scholarships available for individuals with disabilities.
  - In **part 4** of this book I cover more on this topic in detail.

What if Your GPA Gets Too Low?

If it is outlined in your individualized plan that you must have a minimum GPA, it is important to try to maintain it. If it falls below that, the approach taken by VR or WIOA programs can vary. As a general reference, I have often seen the minimum set to be at a 2.0 or 2.5 GPA.

While some programs may have strict GPA requirements — which could result in services / funding being taken away — others may take a more flexible approach and consider various factors before making decisions.

It is essential to communicate openly with your counselor if you encounter challenges with meeting the GPA requirement so that appropriate steps can be taken to support your progress.

Here are some possible scenarios —
- **Review and Adjustment of Individualized Plan**: If your GPA falls below the agreed-upon minimum, your VR or WIOA counselor may review the situation and assess the reasons for the decline. They may discuss potential reasons for the drop in GPA and explore whether any factors related to your disability or other circumstances contributed to the change. Based on the assessment, adjustments to the IPE may occur to better align with your current needs and abilities.
- **Academic Support and Resources**: If your GPA decline is related to academic challenges, your counselor may help you access academic support. Tutoring, study skills workshops, or counseling services are resources to consider. They can provide valuable assistance in improving your academic performance and meeting the requirements of your individualized plan.
- **Progress Monitoring**: Your counselor may implement a monitoring plan to track your progress and academic performance regularly. This may involve periodic check-ins and evaluations to ensure that you are making satisfactory progress toward your vocational goals.
- **Additional Training or Support**: If your vocational goals involve pursuing higher education, your counselor may explore additional training and support services. This could include seeking

accommodation or assistive technology to address specific challenges you may be facing.

- **Re-Evaluation and Adjustment of Goals**: In some cases, if your GPA continues to pose significant challenges in achieving your vocational goals, your counselor may re-evaluate your goals and explore alternative paths or vocational options that better align with your abilities and aspirations.

The primary goal of VR or WIOA programs is to support individuals with disabilities in overcoming barriers to employment and achieving their vocational objectives. So, try to communicate directly with your counselor to avoid defunding.

What If I'm Kicked Out?

If you have been taken out of VR or WIOA, it can be disheartening, but there are steps you can take to address the situation.

- **Request an Explanation**: If you are unsure why you were removed from the VR program, reach out to your counselor or program representative and ask for an explanation. Understanding the reason behind the decision can help you identify areas that need improvement or determine if there was a misunderstanding.
- **Review Your Individualized Plan**: Carefully review your plan to ensure you're meeting the agreed-upon goals and requirements. If you believe that you are following the plan and making progress, discuss this with your VR or WIOA counselor and seek clarification.
- **Petition for Reconsideration**: If you have reason to believe the decision to remove you from the VR or WIOA program was unjustified or based on incorrect information, you may have the option to petition for reconsideration. This typically involves writing a formal letter to the program and providing any necessary evidence or documentation to support your case.
- **Addressing Concerns and Barriers**: If there were specific concerns that led to your removal, work on addressing those issues. This may involve seeking additional support services, addressing academic or vocational challenges, or making adjustments to your vocational goals.
- **Reapply**: In some cases, individuals who were previously removed from the VR or WIOA program may have the opportunity to reapply. Be sure to check with your VR program about their policies on reapplication.
- **Explore Alternative Resources**: If you are unable to rejoin the program consider exploring other support services available in your community that can help you with your vocational goals and employment aspirations.

Change in Health Status?

If your health condition has changed or if you have a new medical condition while receiving VR services, you should take the following steps:

- **Communicate with Your VR Counselor**: Reach out to your VR counselor to inform them about the change in your health condition. Be open and honest about your current situation and how it may impact your vocational goals and services.
- **Reassess Your Vocational Goals**: With the change in your health condition, it's essential to reassess your vocational goals and determine if they need to be adjusted. Discuss with your VR counselor any new career aspirations or modifications to your previous plans.
- **Review Your Individualized Plan**: If you already have an individualized plan in place, review it with your VR counselor to determine if any changes or updates are needed based on your current health status and career objectives.
- **Discuss Service Modifications**: Depending on the changes in your health condition and vocational goals, some services in your IPE may need to be modified or replaced. Work with your VR counselor to identify the appropriate adjustments to ensure that you receive the most relevant and beneficial support. If your condition has become more severe or has new conditions, you might qualify for more services or financial assistance.
- **Complete Any Necessary Documentation**: If your health condition has improved to the point that it no longer substantially impacts your ability to work or pursue education, you may need to provide medical documentation or evidence of your improved condition to update your eligibility status.
- **Explore Other Employment Opportunities**: If your health condition no longer presents a barrier to employment or education, you may want to explore other employment opportunities or career paths that align with your skills, interests, and abilities.

Time Extension and Deferment

"Time Extension for Benefits" or "Deferred Benefits" refers to a provision that allows individuals to extend the duration of their VR or WIOA services beyond the typical time period.

The purpose of a time extension is to provide additional support and services when the standard time frame may not be sufficient. Some reasons for requesting a time extension or deferring benefits could include —

- **Complex Vocational Goals**: If the individual has complex vocational goals that require more time for skill development, educational programs, or training, a time extension may be granted to ensure they have sufficient support.
- **Medical or Personal Circumstances**: Certain medical or personal circumstances may temporarily impede the individual's ability to participate fully in the VR program. A time extension can accommodate these situations and allow the person to resume services when they are better prepared.
- **Change in Circumstances**: Sometimes, unexpected changes in life circumstances may occur during the VR process, warranting additional time to adapt and reassess vocational goals.
- **Educational Delays**: If the individual is pursuing higher education or vocational training, but there are unforeseen delays in completing the program, a time extension may be requested to account for the extended educational timeline.
- **Job Market Challenges**: In cases where the job market is particularly challenging or employment opportunities are limited, a time extension can provide more support in the job search process.

It's important to note that time extensions for benefits are **not automatically granted** and are subject to review and approval by the VR or WIOA office. So, work closely with your VR counselor or WIOA case manager to document the reasons for the request and provide relevant information to support the need for additional time.

Changing Major / Training Focus with VR

If you are selected for the VR program, you must already know what you will major in / study for your educational training.

*However, what if you decide to **change your study focus?***

According to the **U.S. Department of Education**, "Within 3 years of initial enrollment, about 30% of undergraduates in associate's and bachelor's degree programs who had declared a major had changed their major at least once."

With this in mind, if you are currently participating in VR services and decide to change your educational focus, it's important to communicate this decision with your VR counselor **as soon as possible**. Changing your major can impact your individualized plan and the services / support outlined in it. Here's what you should do.

- **Inform Your VR Counselor**: Reach out to your VR counselor to inform them about your decision to change your college major. They need to be aware of the change to assess how it aligns with your vocational goals and make any necessary adjustments to your IPE.
- **Discuss the New Major**: Share the details of your new college major with your VR counselor. Explain why you made the change and how it aligns with your career aspirations. Discuss any additional services or support you may need for the new major.
- **Assess the Impact**: Your VR counselor will evaluate the impact of the major change on your vocational goals and the services provided. They will work with you to determine if any modifications to your IPE are necessary to support your new career path.
- **Reassess Services**: The change in your college major may require adjustments to the services and support provided by VR. This could include modifying educational assistance, vocational training, or other support services based on your new program of study.
- **Address Financial Implications**: Changing your college major may have financial implications, such as changes in tuition costs

or the duration of your education. Work with your VR counselor to understand how these changes may affect your VR benefits.

- **Stay in Communication**: Keep the lines of communication open with your VR counselor throughout the process. Regularly update them on your academic progress and any challenges you may encounter.

- **Seek Career Guidance**: If you're uncertain about the new major's alignment with your career goals, discuss your concerns with your VR counselor. They can provide career guidance and help you make informed decisions.

Finally, if you switch to a **similar training focus** — such as going from one type of engineering to studying a different type of engineering — then that may be a bit easier to communicate and possibly won't require as many adjustments to your individualized plan.

However, pursuing something **completely unrelated** to your original major can potentially be a difficult transition. So, make sure to take that into consideration and consult with your VR counselor **before** you switch majors to see how that would impact the services you receive.

Transferring Schools with VR

If you are part of the VR program and are considering changing schools as a transfer student, it's essential to communicate this decision with your VR counselor as soon as possible. Transferring schools can impact your individualized plan and the VR services and support outlined in it. Here's what you should do:

- **Inform Your VR Counselor:** Reach out to your VR counselor and inform them about your intention to transfer to a different school. Provide them with the reasons for the transfer and any relevant details about the new institution.
- **Discuss the Transfer Plan**: Have a detailed discussion with your VR counselor about your transfer plan. Share information about the new school, the academic program you intend to pursue, and how the transfer aligns with your vocational goals.
- **Assess the Impact**: Your VR counselor will assess how the transfer may impact your vocational goals and the services provided under your IPE. They will work with you to determine if any modifications or adjustments are necessary to continue supporting your career aspirations.
- **Review Educational Services**: If the new school offers different academic programs or services, work with your VR counselor to ensure that your needs are still met. This may include evaluating the compatibility of your new program with your career goals.
- **Address Financial Implications**: Transferring schools may have financial implications, such as changes in tuition costs or other educational expenses. Work with your VR counselor to understand how these changes may affect your VR benefits.
- **Coordinate with New School**: Ensure that the new school is aware of your VR participation and any accommodations or support services you may require as a VR student.
- **Stay in Communication**: Stay in regular communication with your VR counselor throughout the process. Keep them updated on your progress and any challenges you may encounter.
- **Transferring VR Services**: If the new school is in a different state, inquire about transferring your VR services to the new state's VR agency. Your VR counselor can help facilitate this process.

Funding Private vs. Public School

The funding of education by VR agencies can vary depending on whether the college is private or public. Here's how VR funding for education at private and public colleges may differ:

Public Colleges and Universities:
- Public colleges and universities are typically funded by state governments and have lower tuition fees compared to private institutions.
- VR agencies may be more willing to fund education at public colleges because the cost of tuition and fees is generally lower, making it more affordable for the agency.
- VR agencies often have established agreements / partnerships with public colleges, which can facilitate the provision of services and support for students with disabilities.

Private Colleges and Universities:
- Private colleges and universities are funded through private sources, such as tuition fees, donations, and endowments. They tend to have higher tuition costs compared to public institutions.
- VR funding for education at private colleges may be subject to more scrutiny and budget constraints due to the higher cost of attendance.
- When deciding whether to fund education at a private college, VR agencies may consider the student's individual needs, career goals, and the availability of similar programs at public institutions.

If you are considering pursuing education at a private college with the assistance of VR funding, discuss your plans with your VR counselor. They can guide you through the funding process, explain the agency's policies, and help determine the most suitable educational options.

Also, if you happen to have **external financial aid** such as from the FAFSA, scholarships, and so forth — make sure to communicate that with your VR counselor. This in turn might make them more willing to fund the remainder of your educational expenses since VR's financial contribution would be considerably less and more feasible.

Where Does the Money Go & When?

Here's a breakdown of how VR or VIOA funds may be allocated, specifying whether the funds go directly to the educational institution or sent directly to the student:

Funds that might go directly to the educational institution:
- **Tuition and Fees**: Funds may be directly paid to the educational institution to cover the cost of tuition, mandatory fees for vocational training programs, community colleges, technical schools, and universities.
- **Books and Supplies**: Funds may be provided directly to the educational institution's bookstore or credited to the student's account to purchase required textbooks, course materials, and supplies.
- **Training and Certification Programs**: If the student is attending vocational training or certification programs offered by external providers, funds may be paid directly to those providers.

Funds that can be potentially sent directly to the student:
- **Housing:** Funds needed to maintain housing such as at a dorm or apartment.
- **Transportation**: Expenses like public transportation fares or gas expenses, may be provided directly to the student to cover commuting costs.
- **Assistive Technology**: For instance, funds may be provided for a laptop or software to support a student's education.
- **Food**: Many schools offer meal plans that you can potentially use VR funds for, or for groceries if you prefer to prep your own food.
- **Internships and Work Experience**: If a student participates in a job interview, internship or professional workshop, funds may be provided directly to the student to cover transportation or other related expenses, such as paying for professional clothing.
- **Tutoring and Academic Support**: Funds for tutoring or academic support services may be provided directly to the student.
- **Counseling and Career Guidance**: If the student requires counseling services or career guidance, funds may be provided directly to the student to get help.

Additionally, the **individualized plan** provided might outline to a certain extent how funds will be dispersed.

With all that being said, make sure to **request in advance** (a few weeks before the money is needed) to give VR enough time to prepare the funds. It may also be helpful to share with your counselor a timeline of when certain funds may be needed.

Funds are Late?

If you find yourself in a situation where the VR program has not distributed funds in time to cover your education expenses, then here are some steps you can take:

- **Ask for Reimbursement**: If you end up having to pay out of pocket, then ask your VR counselor if they can provide reimbursement for the tuition payment. Explain the situation to your counselor and provide documentation and receipts of the payment you made.
- **Communicate with Your VR Counselor**: Reach out to your VR counselor immediately to inquire about the status of the delayed funding and express your concerns. Sometimes, there could be administrative delays or issues that can be resolved with their intervention.
- **Contact Your School's Financial Aid Office**: Inform the financial aid office at your school about the situation. They may be able to offer you temporary solutions or set up a payment plan while waiting for the VR funds to arrive.
- **Request an Extension**: If possible, ask your school for an extension on the payment deadline and explain that you are waiting for funds from VR to cover the tuition.
- **Follow Up Regularly**: Continue to stay in contact with your VR counselor and the financial aid office to ensure that the funding is being processed.
- **Document Everything**: Keep a record of all communications, emails, and paperwork related to the funding process and tuition payments. Having clear documentation can help in case you need to appeal or resolve any issues in the future.
- **Seek Advocacy Help**: If the situation persists and you are facing significant financial hardship, consider seeking assistance from a disability rights advocate or a local organization that specializes in supporting individuals with disabilities.

VR and Existing Financial Aid

If you already have scholarships and grants to support your college education, it may impact the funding you receive. VR funding is often considered a **secondary funding source**. This means that VR will first look at scholarships, grants, and other benefits. From there, they would attempt to cover that remaining balance.

Also, keep in mind that **financial aid displacement** is a concern that can arise when individuals receive additional funding from sources like VR. This displacement can impact the overall financial support available to the student for their education. For instance, replacing the aid you received from grants and scholarships with the aid received from VR, thus defeating the purpose of having both in the first place.

To avoid displacement and ensure that VR funding complements your existing financial aid package, it's important to take proactive steps and communicate effectively with both the VR agency and the college's financial aid office. Here are some ways to avoid displacement:

- **Inform Both Parties**: Keep your VR counselor and the college's financial aid office informed about the financial aid you have received and any changes in your financial situation. Transparency is essential to ensure that all parties have a complete understanding of your financial needs and the support you are receiving.
- **Explore Reimbursement Options**: If you've already paid for vocational or disability-related expenses out of pocket, discuss the possibility of VR funding providing reimbursements.
- **Fill Out a Cost of Attendance Adjustment Form:** This is typically used to help students avoid displacement of their aid, especially when there are changes in their financial status or educational expenses. To find this *(more so available from colleges)*, simply search for the form's name x your school's name on Google.
- **Rearrange Existing Aid:** If you have a scholarship that allows you to defer the aid to a later semester or year when you need the money more, consider doing so.

VR or Full Scholarship?

Now let's say that you find yourself in a unique situation where you were offered full funding for your education through VR **and** via college financial aid.

Which do you keep? Can you keep both?

I mentioned earlier in the preface of this book that a student in my scholarship **program** had already won $246,000; however, he was also offered full funding from VR.

However, we decided to do a **mix between the two**. Here's why.

Funding Unpredictability:

With scholarships and VR, the funding offered may be prone to changing. For instance, for VR, if you suddenly don't adhere to your individualized plan, you may be let go from the program.

Similar to scholarships, some may require that you have a certain minimum GPA, but if you don't meet that — then you might not receive more funding.

Additionally, some scholarships might be displaced, (replacing free money with free money) thus completely defeating the purpose of winning in the first place. And with VR, there may suddenly be budget constraints that lessen the amount of financial assistance you were initially expecting to get in the future.

So, by using both, it gives you a **backup plan** in case anything goes wrong.

Variating Benefits:

Scholarships may have other benefits you can take advantage of. For example, they may offer internships, job opportunities, exclusive mentorship networks, study abroad stipends, or even offer to cover travel expenses for conferences.

For instance, the family in my **program** *(who inspired this book)* their son was flown out to Los Angeles for a scholarship he won. There he celebrated with other students and learned from industry heads at workshops. Then with a separate scholarship, he and other winners were given free tickets and honored on the field for a National Baseball League team.

Even though with VR, you may not get extravagant experiences, you have the benefit of having a customized plan and assigned professional to help you navigate your education as a student with disabilities. Additionally, VR may fund other expenses that traditional scholarships typically do not — such as assistive technology for accessibility or even for new professional clothing *(such as if you have an upcoming job interview)*.

Conclusion:

For that family, they ended up breaking it up like this:
- Scholarships and grants covered tuition for each school year
- VR covered room and board

So, if you ever find yourself in this situation of having scholarships, grants, and financial assistance offered by VR, take the time to weigh the pros and cons before making a decision.

With that all being said, that concludes part three of this book! Now it's time to learn about scholarships, other money-saving resources, and more.

PART 4: The Alternative Steps - scholarships, grants, money-saving hacks, helpful resources, and more.

The Disabled Debt-Free Degree

By: Carlynn D. Greene

Disability Accommodation Benefits

Academic accommodations are tailored to meet the specific needs of students with disabilities, aiming to provide equitable access to educational opportunities.

Also, keep in mind that you need to **ask in advance** so that everything can be processed and set up in a timely manner. For instance, according to **College Board**, to receive approval in time for the fall semester SAT, students should begin working with their counselor or disability coordinator in the spring of the previous school year well before the summer.

Here are some common examples of academic accommodations for students —

- **Tuition Waivers / Exemptions for Students with Disabilities:** Some colleges offer tuition waivers or exemptions for students with disabilities.
  - For instance, tuition exemption programs specifically for blind and deaf students
  - For a more comprehensive list of waivers / exemptions, simply type in on **Google**; your college's name x the keywords "tuition exemption" or "tuition waiver"
- **Test Waiver:** For many universities, such as graduate schools, they may require you to take the GRE or GMAT. However, my friend with ADHD is currently pursuing a fully funded Ph.D. program that required the GRE, but exempted him from taking it due to his condition. So, reach out to that specific school (or even a scholarship provider that requires a certain test score) telling them about your condition and if an exception can be made.
- **Extended Time**: Allowing extra time for completing exams, quizzes, or assignments, for students with processing or reading difficulties. This can particularly be beneficial for taking major tests such as the **SAT**, **ACT**, **GRE**, **GMAT**, **MCAT**, **AP**, **CLEP** etc. More time might help you feel more comfortable during the exam in order to potentially score better.

- **Distraction-Free Environment**: Providing a quiet and isolated space for students who have difficulty concentrating in a typical classroom setting.
- **Prerequisite Course Exemption**: Opting out from taking certain classes that may be required for your study concentration.
    - For instance, students with dyslexia or language processing disorders may be eligible to opt out of foreign language requirements due to language challenges.
- **Flexible Attendance Policies**: Providing flexibility in attendance requirements for students with chronic health conditions or disabilities may affect regular class attendance.
- **Alternative Testing Methods**: Offering alternative ways to demonstrate knowledge, such as oral exams or presentations, for students who may have difficulty with traditional written exams.
- **Priority Registration**: Allowing students with disabilities to register early for courses to secure accommodations and create a more manageable schedule. This is extremely helpful since many courses fill up fast, especially for an underclassman. Often schools open class registration in order of seniority and a lot of times freshmen get waitlisted for courses.
- **Modified Assignments**: Making modifications to assignments or tests, such as reducing the number of questions or providing different types of assessments, for specific learning needs.
- **Use of Assistive Technology**: Providing assistive technology like screen readers, speech recognition software, or digital textbooks can support students with visual, hearing, or learning disabilities. This is helpful since some professors may have a "no technology policy" but you would rather take digital notes.
- **Preferential Seating**: Allowing students to sit closer to the front of the classroom to hear and see the instructor or board better.
- **Note-Taking Assistance**: Access to class notes, either through a note-taker or digital copies. This would benefit students with difficulty taking notes due to physical or cognitive challenges.

If for whatever reason you are having difficulty with getting these accommodations after requesting them yourself, then have your VR counselor or related disability advocates call your school administrators to advocate for you on your behalf.

Contacting Higher Education Authority

Contacting your state's higher education authority (HEA) can also potentially be beneficial when seeking medical-based financial aid.

To contact your state's HEA for medical-based financial aid, use **this link** and select your state or territory. From there, reach out to your state's "Higher Education Agency." Here are some more ways in which they may assist you.

- **Access to Financial Aid:** If you are a student with a disability and encounter challenges accessing federal or state financial aid programs, your state's higher education authority can provide guidance and assistance in navigating the financial aid application process.
- **Inaccessible Facilities:** If you encounter physical barriers or inaccessible facilities on your college campus, such as a lack of ramps, elevators, or accessible restrooms, you can contact the state authority to report these issues and advocate for necessary improvements.
- **Accommodations Disputes:** If you face challenges in obtaining reasonable accommodations for your disability from your college or university, the state higher education authority can help mediate disputes and ensure that your rights under disability laws, such as the Americans with Disabilities Act (ADA) and Section 504 of the Rehabilitation Act, are upheld.
- **Discrimination or Harassment:** If you experience harassment, discrimination, or unequal treatment on the basis of your disability, the state authority can provide guidance on how to file a complaint and seek resolution.
- **Advocacy and Support**: In cases where you face challenges or need accommodations, the higher education authority may be able to advocate on your behalf or direct you to resources for support.
- **Referrals to Support Services**: Higher education authorities often have partnerships with various organizations and support services that cater to students with medical conditions. They can provide referrals and recommendations to help you access additional resources.

Job Hack for Disabilities

Through Schedule A, individuals with disabilities have the opportunity to work in various federal agencies and departments in the United States through a **non-competitive process**. This means they may be hired for the job without being required to go through the traditional competitive hiring process.

Some examples of places to work through **Schedule A include:**
- National Aeronautics and Space Administration (NASA)
- Department of Health and Human Services (HHS)
- Department of Education (ED)
- Department of Justice (DOJ)
- Environmental Protection Agency (EPA)
- Federal Communications Commission (FCC)
- U.S. Census Bureau
- U.S. Department of Agriculture (USDA)
- Department of Veterans Affairs (VA)
- And more

Many of these jobs can be found on the **USA Jobs** website. However, not all agencies use this site to showcase job vacancies, so it is important to check specific government agency websites such as those seen **here** for additional open applications. For more advice regarding this process, refer to **this publication** from the U.S. Equal Employment Opportunity Commission.

The Schedule A program offers several benefits to individuals with disabilities seeking **federal** job opportunities such as —

- **Hiring Preferences**: Schedule A provides individuals with disabilities priority consideration for federal job openings. This creates an advantage over other applicants who do not qualify under this hiring authority.
- **Opportunities for Career Advancement**: Being hired through Schedule A provides individuals with disabilities the opportunity to build a career within the federal government. Once hired, they have the chance to demonstrate their abilities and potentially advance in their careers.

- **Reasonable Accommodations**: Federal agencies are required to provide reasonable accommodations to individuals with disabilities to ensure they can perform their job duties effectively. This commitment to accessibility promotes an inclusive and supportive work environment.
- **Federal Benefits and Stability**: Federal employees may receive various benefits, including health insurance, retirement plans, paid leave, and job security. This stability and comprehensive benefits package make federal employment an attractive option.
- **Supportive Work Environment**: Many federal agencies have initiatives and programs in place to support employees with disabilities and create an inclusive workplace culture.

Finally, there are also other platforms out there dedicated to those with disabilities to find jobs. For instance, **AbilityJobs.com** has a database of jobs to apply to and even career fairs throughout the year you could attend. They strive for accessibility and have:
- Sign language Interpreters on-call to assist with live meetings
- Real-time talk-to-text captions for people with hearing difficulties

Also, there's **Inclusively** and **Getting Hired**. With these platforms, you can connect to jobs and receive curated job matches from employers who are committed to disability inclusion and creating diverse teams.

Scholarship Databases

There are many scholarship websites out there. However, some may be better than others with opportunities listed, their user interface, filters you can use, etc. Here are some to consider using.

United States —
Scholarship databases I recommend include:
- **GoingMerry.com**
  - Create a free profile here. They have a feature that enables you to bulk apply to certain scholarships, saving you time! Additionally, they have a mobile app that will auto-input general information for future scholarships
- **Bold.org**
  - This is where I host the scholarships I personally **give out!** I suggest you create a free profile here as well because their scholarships can only be applied to via their platform.
  - If you have difficulty creating an account on this platform (more often happens for U.S. international students), then **contact** their email to help with getting it set up.
- **Profellow.com**
  - Here you can find various fully funded graduate programs for a master's / doctoral degree.

Canada —
For general Canadian scholarship databases, use these websites:
- **scholarshipscanada.com**
- **Studentawards.com**
- **scholartree.ca**

There is even a scholarship database specific to finding scholarships available across Canada specifically for students with disabilities:
- **Disabilityawards.ca**

For **other countries / continents** or databases that list many **study abroad / international student** opportunities, simply refer to this PDF I put together:
- **Download PDF here**

Scholarship & College Application Tips

As a student with disabilities, standing out in scholarships or even college admissions applications require emphasizing your unique strengths, experiences, and achievements. Here are some tips to help you make your application stand out:

- **Highlight Your Achievements**: Showcase your academic accomplishments, extracurricular activities, and leadership roles. Highlight any honors, awards, or recognition you have received.
- **Emphasize Your Resilience**: Share your journey of overcoming challenges and how you have persevered in the face of adversity. If you feel comfortable doing so, feel free to share how your disability has shaped you into who you are today.
- **Tell Your Story**: Use your personal statement to share your personal story, experiences, and aspirations. Be authentic and honest about how your disability has influenced your academic and personal growth.
- **Focus on Your Goals**: Clearly articulate your educational and career goals. Explain how receiving the scholarship will help you achieve those goals and make a positive impact on your community.
- **Demonstrate Your Involvement**: Highlight any community service or advocacy activities. It really helps to show how you were, are, and plan to continue being involved in helping others.
- **Provide Strong Recommendations**: Request letters of recommendation from teachers, mentors, or community leaders who can speak to your abilities, determination, and potential.
- **Customize Your Application**: Tailor each scholarship application to the specific criteria and mission of the scholarship provider. Show how you align with their values and goals.
- **Seek Assistance from Disability Services**: If your school has a disability services office, they may offer guidance and support with scholarship applications. They can help you identify scholarships specifically designed for students with disabilities.
- **Submit Accommodations Requests**: If needed, request reasonable accommodations for the application process, such as extended deadlines or alternative formats.

- **Edit and Proofread**: Carefully review your application to ensure it is error-free and well-written. Consider seeking feedback from teachers or advisors. I also offer an **essay editing** service.
- **Express Gratitude**: If possible, follow up with a thank-you note after submitting your application. Showing gratitude can leave a positive impression.

Additionally, I wanted to give you an example of how to effectively write a **scholarship essay**. Below is an **essay excerpt** from a **student** in my scholarship **program** who won **24 scholarships** during her junior and senior years of college.

Yes, you read that right! She won that many even as an upperclassman and graduated from college **debt-free** in August of 2023. This just goes to show that it is never too late to apply and win! In her essay, she discussed her medical condition as it relates to why she was pursuing her study concentration in medical laboratory science:

"If one new perspective was revealed to me during this period of my life, it was that one's disability shouldn't overshadow the opportunities they are given. As a Medical Laboratory Scientist, I strive to become a researcher, studying severely underrepresented, chronic conditions in the immunological field. I would love to focus on the science behind why food intolerances occur and how these can influence gut-brain interactions. Eventually, I want to expand into the non-profit realm and provide sensitivity testing to patients in areas where these services aren't typically available. I am prepared to make my own seat at the table if there isn't one already — and advocate for our communities that face the most disparities in healthcare."

Also, here is the **testimonial video** from a student in my program who won the Taco Bell Live Mas scholarship. He is on the **Autism spectrum**. We went through **five rounds of revisions** for his winning video.

Scholarships are **very strategic**. It's not just a matter of filling out the application, scoring well on standardized tests, and hoping for the best. It's important to **be intentional** with **which ones you apply** to and **how you execute the** overall application.

General Disability Scholarships

As a **disclaimer**, some scholarships listed may have deadlines that have already passed. If it reopens, then please remember to apply by **taking note** of it on your **scholarship list**. Create a copy via Google and use this **template** I made to start your own spreadsheet of scholarships.

Below you will find some general disability scholarships. Of course, this is not a full list — however, it should give you an idea of what's out there! Also, within this **PDF**, I put together an **even longer listing** that is organized as follows:

- State-specific Disability Scholarships
- Mental Disability Scholarships
- Physical Disability Scholarships
- Hearing Impairment Scholarships
- Visual Impairment / Blind Scholarships
- Learning Disability Scholarships
- Autism Scholarships
- Cancer Scholarships
- Down Syndrome Scholarships

To find even more funding opportunities for specific disabilities use this **search engine** from Needy Meds and search by the alphabet letter of your condition.

Wells Fargo Scholarship Program for People with Disabilities
Eligibility: The bank Wells Fargo offers scholarships to students who have an identified disability. Applicants must also be high school seniors, high school graduates, or college undergraduates who plan to enroll in full- or half-time undergraduate study at an accredited United States two- or four-year college or university for the upcoming academic year.

> (*The 24x student winner mentioned in the previous chapter won this scholarship as well!*)

Microsoft Disability Scholarship
Eligibility: This scholarship will be awarded to promising high school seniors with disabilities who plan to attend a vocational or academic college and aspire to have a career in the technology industry. The scholarships are renewable.

Google-Lime Scholarship

Eligibility: Offered by The Lime Network in partnership with Google, this award is for students with disabilities pursuing a computer science or computer engineering degree in the U.S. ($10,000) or Canada ($5,000).

AAHD Scholarship Program

Eligibility: Applicant must be enrolled as a full-time undergraduate student and must have completed one full year of college or more. Applicants must have a disability and provide documentation to verify this.

Auger & Auger Disabled Scholar Award

Eligibility: For disabled undergraduate students. Applicants must write a personal essay about overcoming their disability and the lessons learned. Deadlines are in July and November.

Test Prep Insight $1,500 Scholarship

Applicants must be currently enrolled at or planning to attend a two to four year university, community college, or graduate school program located in the United States. Candidates must have a medically recognized physical or mental disability with a minimum of a 2.5 GPA.

The Frederick J. Krause Scholarship on Health and Disability

Eligibility: This scholarship provides financial assistance to students with disabilities planning to attend vocational or academic college and pursue a career in the technology industry.

Mays Mission for the Handicapped Scholarship Program

Eligibility: This scholarship is for students with physical or mental disabilities pursuing vocational training in a four-year undergraduate program. A minimum GPA of 2.3 is required.

Buckfire & Buckfire P.C. Disability Scholarship Program

Eligibility: This scholarship is for students with physical, mental, learning, or psychiatric disabilities attending college or university. Applicants must submit documentation of their disability and an essay.

Gabriel's Foundation of HOPE College Scholarship

Eligibility: For students with disabilities or those with a family member with a disability who want to work for the benefit of disabled people. A personal essay and two letters of reference are required.

AIM Center for Independent Living Scholarship

Eligibility: Applicants must have a documented disability and be pursuing an associate's or bachelor's degree at an accredited college or university or enrolled in a recognized vocational/trade school.

The Susanna and Lucy DeLaurentis Scholarships

Eligibility: For college-bound high school seniors with a disability.

Once again — make sure to refer to the PDF and search engine mentioned earlier in this chapter for disability scholarships that are more specific to certain conditions!

Studying Abroad Scholarships

Studying abroad as someone with a disability can be challenging, but that doesn't always mean it is not possible.

When I visited Japan and South Korea to promote a study abroad company, I interviewed a student with cerebral palsy. View my study abroad video where she is featured in it **here**.

That was in fact ***her third time being in Japan*** — and she loved it! And I especially appreciated how the staff members of the company went above and beyond for accommodations, diet restrictions, and more.

The study abroad company I partnered with also **has scholarships**. Their **diversity scholarship** is open to those with disabilities. Also, here's another study abroad company's **disability grant.**

There's even the **Holman Prize for Blind Ambition** which offers up to $25,000 for three visually impaired individuals to explore the world and push their limits.

This one is not specific to people with disabilities, but you should still consider it. The **Boren Awards** funds opportunities for U.S. citizen undergraduate and graduate students to study abroad in regions critical to U.S. national security interests. The main programs under the Boren Awards are the Boren Scholarships (undergraduates) and the Boren Fellowships (graduates). I had a student win this award for $25,000.

For more study abroad / international student resources, use:
- **globalscholarships.com**
- **diversityabroad.com**

According to this news **article** from NBC, these are the **most physically accessible cities** in the world (as rated by those with disabilities). Some of these include:
- Shanghai (China), Tokyo (Japan), Amsterdam (Netherlands), Paris (France), London (England, UK), Sydney (Australia), Las Vegas (Nevada, USA)

However, always do **more research** outside of this! Levels of accessibility may be different depending on certain disabilities and of course intersectionality of identities which can impact experience as well.

Also regarding the student I mentioned earlier who has cerebral palsy — there were certain moments when she had to walk instead of using her electric wheelchair. Japan has many areas that are very narrow such as local shops and restaurants. Or even how at traditional Japanese shrines, the stone ground was very unleveled and not paved which is not ideal for a wheelchair.

So, if you have a physical disability, make sure to take into consideration the physical accessibility of certain countries, specific cities, excursion sites, school campuses, and housing accommodations.

Study Abroad Advice

Now that I have covered some ways to obtain funding for studying abroad, here are some steps to take if you wish to study abroad and how to advocate for yourself.

- **Research Study Abroad Programs**: Begin by researching study abroad programs that offer support and accommodations for students with disabilities. Look for programs that have experience working with students with the same or similar disabilities and have a commitment to accessibility.
- **Contact Disability Services**: Reach out to the study abroad office or disability services office at your home institution. Also, attend informational sessions and ask lots of questions. They can provide valuable info about available programs, resources, and the application process. They may also be able to connect you with other students who have studied abroad with disabilities.
- **Disclose Your Disability**: It is essential to disclose your disability to both your home institution AND the study abroad program. This allows them to make necessary accommodations and support arrangements during your time abroad.
- **Research Accessibility**: Investigate the accessibility of your chosen destination, including public transportation, buildings, and facilities. Look for information about wheelchair and housing accessibility, and other accommodations you may require. Ask yourself what accessible housing looks like for you and identify your needs. Request, if possible, a virtual tour of certain places (such as what a typical dorm may look like).
- **Accommodation Plans**: Discuss your specific accommodation needs with the study abroad program and the host institution. This may include accessible housing, sign language interpreters, assistive technology, or any other accommodations required to support your academic and daily living needs.
- **Cultural Awareness and Communication:** Familiarize yourself with the culture and attitudes towards disabilities in your host country. Learn about disability-related laws and rights and be prepared to communicate your needs and preferences clearly.
- **Insurance and Medical Considerations**: Ensure that you have adequate health insurance coverage while studying abroad.

Review and discuss your healthcare options and all resources while abroad and use them. Research medical facilities and resources in your host country and consider any special medical needs or prescriptions.

- **Cultural Awareness and Communication**: Familiarize yourself with the culture and attitudes towards disabilities in your host country. Learn about disability-related laws and rights and be prepared to communicate your needs and preferences clearly.
- **Language Skills**: Research beforehand what language(s) that country primarily speaks and if the study abroad program you're interested in offers courses primarily in your native language or not. The study abroad company I partnered with offered courses to students in English. So, there wasn't as much of a need to already know another language. However, having a general understanding of that country's language is always beneficial. In addition, using translation apps can translate based on pictures you take from your phone. I used this a lot for translating public transit signs and food menus!
- **Prepare for Emergencies:** Have a plan in place for handling emergencies like seeking assistance for disability-related issues or medical emergencies. Have plenty of medication equipment such as batteries for an electric wheelchair, EpiPens, inhalers, etc.
- **Support Network**: Establish a support network before and during your time abroad. This can include friends, family, local contacts, and any organizations or groups that support students with disabilities in your host country.
- **Consider Having a Personal Care Assistant**: The student I mentioned earlier had with her a person there to support her.

Finally, here is some **more advice** for studying abroad with disabilities:
- **Resource 1**
- **Resource 2**
- **Resource 3**
- **Resource 4**
- **Resource 5**

Disability Student Loan Forgiveness

Automatic discharge of student loans is a type of **student loan forgiveness.** This discharge is known as a "Total and Permanent Disability (TPD) Discharge." There are certain situations in which individuals with disabilities may be eligible for an automatic discharge of their federal student loans such as for those who have:

- Federal Perkins Loans
- William D. Ford Federal Direct Loan (**Direct Loan**) Program loans
- Federal Family Education Loan (**FFEL**) Program loans
- If you received a **TEACH Grant**, a TPD discharge also relieves you of your TEACH Grant service obligation.

According to **StudentAid.gov**, as of May 2023, around 492,000 borrowers have gotten loan forgiveness through TPD discharge.

Those who qualify must **meet** at least **one** of three criteria:

- **Social Security Disability:** Borrowers may qualify for discharge by providing documentation from the Social Security Administration (SSA). They must show that they are receiving Social Security Disability Insurance (SSDI) or Supplemental Security Income (SSI) benefits based on their disability.
- **Veterans**: Veterans can qualify for a TPD discharge if they have a service-connected disability and have been determined to be unemployable by the Department of Veterans Affairs (VA).
- **Medical Professional Certification:** Borrowers may also qualify based on certification from a medical professional (who is licensed to practice in the U.S.) to certify Section 4 of your TPD application that they have a total and permanent disability. The medical professional's certification has to show that you are "unable to engage in any substantial *gainful activity*." (*This means that you can't perform work for pay that involves doing significant physical or mental activities, or a combination of both.*) Secondly, the medical professional must confirm that your inability to engage in substantial gainful activity is **because** of a physical or mental disability that can be — expected to result in death; **OR** has lasted for a continuous period of at least 5 years (60 months); **OR** can be expected to last for a continuous period

of at least 5 years (60 months). Here are the **types of medical professionals** who can certify your disability for TPD discharge:
- ○ Doctor of Medicine (MD)
- ○ Doctor of osteopathy/osteopathic medicine (DO)
- ○ Nurse practitioner (NP)
- ○ Physician's assistant (PA)
- ○ Certified psychologist at the independent practice level

If a borrower meets the eligibility criteria for a Total and Permanent Disability Discharge, they will not be required to make further loan payments, and any outstanding balance on their federal student loans will be discharged.

And in the case that you fully or partially recover from your medical condition that was previously deemed total and permanent — you can still go back to school even after you had a discharge of your student loans. You would have to give a letter from your doctor stating that you are once again able to engage in substantial gainful activity.

For more information regarding the TPD process, use this **link**.

To apply use this **link**.

It's important to note that the process for obtaining a TPD discharge can vary based on the borrower's specific circumstances and the type of documentation required. Borrowers should contact their loan servicer or the U.S. Department of Education for guidance on the application process and required documentation.

Finally, did you know that there are even **scholarships for paying off student loan debt?** I even personally give out one! You can find a list of such opportunities within my **free financial aid toolkit.**

General Disability Opportunities

Here are some more resources to consider looking into.

AccessibleGO: Offers travel deals for individuals with disabilities. Free access to their platform includes thousands of discounts for hotels, flights, cruises, attractions, rental cars, and informative travel resources.

Computers with Causes: Provides free computers to students with disabilities. The organization works with schools and individual services to offer refurbished computers to those in need.

Special Needs Alliance: This national alliance of **attorneys** helps families plan for the future. Attorneys specialize in public benefits, trust and tax planning, and legal issues for individuals with disabilities. The website includes educational information on tax-free savings accounts, accessing special education services, and establishing special needs trusts.

U.S. Department of Agriculture: USDA provides grant and loan funding for individuals and families seeking assistance with home renovations or repairs. USDA offers financial support for people with disabilities, older adults, and low-income individuals.

Volunteers of America: VOA provides housing assistance, and specialized employment services to people with disabilities, for elderly housing, multi-family housing, and more.

Friends of Disabled Adults and Children: FODAC offers medical equipment to individuals with disabilities at little or no cost. The nonprofit provides services to people of all ages, no matter their financial status.

Achieving a Better Life Experience (ABLE) accounts: ABLE accounts allow eligible people with disabilities to save money to pay for "qualified disability expenses" (QDEs). **QDEs include:**
- Education and training
- Basic living expenses
- Health and wellness expenses
- Housing

- Financial management
- Transportation
- Assistive technology
- Legal fees
- And other expenses

In the context of being a student, ABLE accounts allow families to save for the education of students with disabilities and pay for qualified disability-related expenses without affecting eligibility for government assistance programs.

According to the **IRS**, "Earnings in an ABLE account aren't taxed unless a distribution exceeds a designated beneficiary's qualified disability expenses." It's also important to note that contributions to ABLE accounts aren't deductible for federal tax purposes.

To learn more about ABLE accounts, use this **link**.

Disability Benefit Programs

SSI (Supplemental Security Income) and **SSDI** (Social Security Disability Insurance) are both disability benefit programs provided by the Social Security Administration (SSA) in the U.S.

Both programs **provide financial assistance** to disabled individuals by offering **monthly payments to those in the program**. To give you an idea of these payments, here is some more information —

- **SSI**: The monthly maximum federal amounts for 2023 are $914 for an eligible individual, $1,371 for an eligible individual with an eligible spouse, and $458 for an essential person.
- **SSDI**: As of 2023, the average disability benefit per month is $1,483, with a maximum of $3,627/month for those who retire at full retirement age.

Other benefits of qualifying —

- **Food Assistance**: Qualification often automatically makes someone eligible for SNAP benefits, aka food stamps.
- **Free Phone Service**: Through **Q Link Wireless**, you might qualify for free monthly data, talk, & text. This is thanks to the government programs, **Lifeline Program (LP)** and **Affordable Connection Program (ACP).**
  - For **ACP** specifically, students who receive the **Pell Grant** via the FAFSA are also eligible.
- **Housing Assistance**: Disabled individuals may be eligible for housing assistance programs like Section 8, which provides subsidized rental housing to low-income households.
  - **NOTE**: There are also **housing scholarships** for those under Section 8 / Public Housing. Check within your state!
- **Energy Assistance:** The Low-Income Home Energy Assistance Program (LIHEAP) offers financial assistance to help eligible individuals with their home energy bills.
- **Legal Aid:** Disabled individuals may have access to free or low-cost legal services through legal aid organizations.

Who is eligible?

In summary, **SSDI** is for individuals who have paid into the Social Security system and have a qualifying work history.

Whereas **SSI** is intended for low-income individuals who are 65 years old or older, are blind, or have a qualifying disability. Though alike in various ways, they have different eligibility requirements and benefit structures. To learn more about both, then use this **link**.

Children under age 18 can get **SSI** if they meet Social Security's **definition** of disability for children. Also, if you are participating in an approved program of special education, VR, or similar services, your benefits may **continue** even after you are 18-years-old.

Additionally, there's the Student Earned Income Exclusion **(SEIE).** This is a provision that allows certain **SSI** recipients (must be under the age of 22 and attending school) to exclude a portion of their earned income when determining their SSI benefit amount. This exclusion allows students to earn income without affecting their SSI benefits significantly. It is designed to encourage SSI recipients to pursue education or vocational training while still receiving necessary financial support.

Under **SSI** there's also the Plan for Achieving Self Support (**PASS**). A provision to help individuals with disabilities return to work. PASS helps people set aside money for purchases, installment, and down payments. Additionally for things like vehicles, wheelchairs, or a computer if needed to reach their vocational goal. A VR counselor can help with setting this process up.

To learn more about **PASS**, use this **link**.

To learn more about **employment-related provisions of** SSI and SSDI programs, refer to the **Red Book**.

If denied for SSI or SSDI — here's what you need to know and do.

According to the Social Security Administration's 2021 **annual report**, "Denied disability claims have averaged **67%**" and most of which happened due to **technical denials**. The odds of getting approved or denied also vary greatly depending on which **state** you are in. To better visualize this and see your specific state, refer to this **publication**.

To learn various other reasons why your application might be denied, refer to **this post** from a disability law firm.

In the case of being **denied**, you can **appeal the decision.** In many cases, you have the right to appeal a denial. The appeal process generally consists of the following stages —

- **Request for Reconsideration**: This is the first level of appeal. You must file a written request for reconsideration within 60 days of receiving the denial letter. The SSA will have a different person review your application.
- **Hearing With a Judge**: If your request for reconsideration is also denied, you can request a hearing before an administrative law judge. Do so within 60 days of the reconsideration denial.
- **Appeals Council**: If the judge's decision is unfavorable, you can request a review by the SSA's Appeals Council.
- **Federal Court**: If all else fails, file a federal district court action with the U.S. District Court if you don't agree with the response from the Appeals Council.

Furthermore, consider consulting with a local disability attorney or advocate. Many people find it helpful to consult with those who specialize in SSDI / SSI cases. They can provide expert guidance, help gather evidence, and navigate various medical situations.

To locate them, use the links provided below:
- **Find** a **medical advocate** in your state
- **Find** a **disability attorney** in your state

In conclusion, there are so many ways that those with disabilities can benefit financially. I know that all this information at once may be overwhelming to understand at first.

So, reread through this chapter at a separate time and reach out to someone who has expertise relating to SSI and SSDI. Contact your **local Social Security office** to inform you of benefits within your state. Ask them for guidance on how to apply, and so forth.
- Use this **link** to locate a **Social Security office near you.**

Parents With and Without Disabilities Benefits

Parents with and without disabilities may have specific statuses that enable their student to qualify for certain assistance programs. The availability of these benefits can vary depending on the country and region, as well as the specific disability and financial circumstances. Here are some potential benefits that parents with disabilities may be eligible for to support their college-bound or college-enrolled children.

- **Financial Aid and Scholarships**: Parents with disabilities can explore government-funded grants, loans, and scholarships that may be applicable to their children's education. Here are some to consider applying to primarily based in the United States:
  - **Disabled Parent Scholarships**
  - **Child of Deaf Parents Scholarship** (*open to any nation, no citizenship requirement*)
- **Tuition Exemptions and Waivers**: Some schools will make your child's education tuition-free if —
  - They are the children of disabled or deceased firefighters or law enforcement officers
  - A child of a veteran missing in action
  - If you perhaps work for that specific school
  - If the child is adopted, was in foster care, etc.
  - Check with the schools your child is applying to (or currently enrolled at) to see what specific benefits are outlined. To do so, search for on Google: **[school name] x "tuition exemption" or "tuition waiver"**
- **Employer Benefits**: Some employers offer education assistance programs or scholarships for their employees and their dependents, including children.
- **Unions**: Some labor or credit unions (some banks as well) may have exclusive opportunities for their members with benefits that can extend to their children (like scholarships).
- **State or Regional Assistance Programs**: Certain regions / states may have specific resources aimed at supporting college-bound or college-enrolled students with disabilities.
- **Private and Nonprofit Support**: Disability-specific organizations or charitable foundations may provide financial assistance or

scholarships to support college students with disabilities and their families.

- **VR Services**: In some places, VR services may extend to the children of individuals with disabilities. The chances increase if the parent's disability affects their ability to financially support their child's education. These services may include financial assistance for education-related expenses. Again, this is **not** a universal benefit, so check with your VR counselor.
- **Social Security Disability Benefits**: Some countries provide disability benefits, including SSI or SSDI, that may offer financial assistance to disabled parents with college-bound children.
- **Tax Credits and Deductions**: Tax benefits such as child tax credits or education-related deductions may be available to parents with disabilities to help offset college expenses.

In conclusion, eligibility criteria, application processes, and available benefits can vary significantly. Consult with government agencies, financial aid offices, or disability support organizations to better understand the full range of assistance options available.

Intellectual Disability Resource

Now let's talk about comprehensive transition and postsecondary (CTP) programs.

As seen from the **StudentAid.gov** website —
- A CTP program for students with an intellectual disability (ID) is a degree, certificate, or non-degree program that is offered by a college or career school and approved by the U.S. Department of Education.
- CTP programs are designed to support students with ID who want to continue academic, career, and independent living instruction. The goal is to prepare for gainful employment.
- Those within CTP programs are offered academic advising and a structured curriculum.
- To determine your eligibility, you would have to contact the financial aid office at your college or career school.

Where to find CTP and ID-inclusive schools?
Think College features information on over 300 postsecondary schools that have programs or overall institutions specifically for students with an ID. Not all schools listed have a CTP program, but many do. They also have a search filter specifically for CTP programs.

Additionally, they have provided a **guide** listing over 50 questions to ask college programs as someone with an ID.

Here are some of the benefits CTP programs offer —
- **Individualized Supports**: For instance, accommodations tailored to the unique needs of each student. These supports can include academic tutoring, counseling, career guidance, and assistive technology.
- **Skill Development**: They focus on developing essential life skills and vocational skills, such as communication, problem-solving, time management, and job readiness. Overall, the program helps students succeed in their academic pursuits and future careers.
- **Increased Employment Opportunities**: By participating in CTP programs, students gain valuable skills and experiences that can enhance their employability. CTP programs often include

internships and work-based learning opportunities to prepare students for the workforce.

- **Transition to Employment**: CTP programs have a strong emphasis on transitioning students from school to employment. They work with local employers to create job opportunities and support students in finding and maintaining meaningful employment.
- **Social Inclusion**: These programs foster a supportive and inclusive learning environment, promoting social integration and friendships among students with and without disabilities.
- **Increased Independence**: CTP aims to empower students with intellectual disabilities to become more independent in their daily lives. This includes managing their finances, transportation, and decision-making.
- **Advocacy and Support**: They often have dedicated staff and advisors who provide ongoing advocacy and support for students to ensure they have a positive and successful college experience.

Free or Cheaper Medical Expenses

Cheaper Prescription Medication:

Cost Plus Drugs, launched January of 2022 its online pharmacy. It was started by Mark Cuban, owner of the Dallas Mavericks NBA team, and one of the *Shark Tank* judges. The company was created because they believed Americans should have access to safe and affordable medicines. Their pharmacy cuts out the middlemen to offer many common generic medications at wholesale prices.

Some people have seen the price of their usual medication go from costing **thousands** of dollars, to just a **few dollars** by switching to this platform. You can see **here**, and in the screenshot below, *(dated as of August 31, 2023)* just how much the **retail price vs. their price** is for certain medications:

Medication	Form	Retail price ▾	Our price	Savings
Fingolimod HCl (Generic for Gilenya)	Bottle of Capsules	$13,067.14	$295.03	Save $12,772.11
Penicillamine (Generic for Cuprimine)	Capsule	$11,192.10	$135.20	Save $11,056.90
Tolvaptan (Generic for Samsca)	Tablet	$9,039.90	$1,902.50	Save $7,137.40
Teriflunomide (Generic for Aubagio)	Tablet	$3,552.30	$12.80	Save $3,539.50

- Watch this **interview** with Mark Cuban on why he started this and how it works in comparison to other pharmaceutical companies.

Negotiating & Lowering Medical Bills:

Many do not realize that sometimes medical bills can be **negotiated**. You can request for an **"itemized bill."** It is **estimated** that up to **80% of medical bills have errors.**

I wish I had known this when I broke my teeth and jaw from a biking accident on my college campus. A five-minute ride in the ambulance to the hospital *(where I wasn't hooked up to anything)* plus the stitches and painkillers cost me over $1,000 … *Yikes.*

If this is new information to you and you have already paid your medical bill, you might be able to **still request a refund** for a medical payment. Especially if you later discover that the bill was incorrect.

However, keep in mind that the **time limit** for requesting a refund for a medical payment can vary depending on the policies of the medical provider or the healthcare facility. It's essential to **act promptly** and submit your refund request as soon as you discover an error or discrepancy in the billing.

With that being said, here's how to start this process whether that's before or after you already paid the medical bill —

- **Contact the Billing Department:** Reach out to the hospital or healthcare provider's billing department either by phone or in person. Explain that you would like an itemized bill that breaks down the charges for the medical services you received.
- **Request an Itemized Bill:** Politely request a detailed breakdown of all the charges on your bill. Ask for a line-by-line explanation of each service, procedure, medication, and any other expenses included in the bill.
- **Review the Itemized Bill**: Once you receive the itemized bill, carefully review each charge to ensure accuracy. Look for any duplicate charges, services you didn't receive, or any other errors that may have inflated the total cost.
- **Identify Discrepancies:** If you find any discrepancies or questionable charges, contact the billing department again to discuss these specific items. Ask for clarification and provide any relevant documentation or proof that supports your case.
- **Negotiate or Request Adjustments:** If you believe certain charges are inaccurate or unreasonable, try negotiating with the billing department to lower the costs. You can present evidence of average costs for similar medical services or inquire about any available discounts or financial assistance programs.
- **Be Persistent and Polite:** Dealing with medical billing can be challenging, but it's essential to remain persistent and polite throughout the process. Keep records of all conversations, names of people you've spoken to, and any agreements reached.

- **Ask about Financial Assistance**: According to the **Washington Post**, "If there was no mistake with your bill, but you cannot afford to pay it, check into financial assistance. Under the Affordable Care Act, hospitals are required to have **financial assistance policies**. If you meet certain income requirements, you may qualify for financial assistance programs, often called 'charity care'. These programs may allow your bill to be **canceled in whole or partially**. If you are uninsured, ask for a **self-pay or cash discount**. If you are not eligible for charity care, set up a payment plan."
    - To find financial assistance with your hospital, it's easier to simply Google: **the name of the hospital x "financial assistance"**
    - Read the **full article** from the Washington Post for additional advice relating to this process.
- **Seek Help from a Patient / Billing Advocate Group**: If you encounter difficulties or feel overwhelmed with the process, consider seeking help from a patient or medical billing advocate. They provide support, information, and assistance to individuals who are facing challenges with medical billing and insurance-related issues.
    - **Umbra Health Advocacy** and the **National Association of Healthcare Advocacy** both have a searchable directory of advocates or case managers near you.
    - To determine if an individual patient advocate is right for you, refer to **this blog** on how to interview and choose.

General Grants to Offset Medical Expenses:

- **HealthWell Foundation**: This non-profit organization offers financial assistance to eligible individuals who have difficulty paying for medical treatments and expenses.
- **Patient Advocate**: This platform offers financial aid grants to help offset medical expenses. Additionally, they have a **National Financial Resource Directory** to help individuals quickly generate a list of national / regional resources more specific to certain conditions.

Medical Condition-specific Financial Assistance:

Many condition-specific organizations provide financial assistance programs for patients with certain medical conditions. Search for foundations related to your condition to see if they offer grants.

I also recommend applying for financial assistance from these organizations that are **state-specific** so that the pool of applicants is significantly less, and you are **more likely** to be given the funds.

For instance, when I typed in on Google, "Texas leukemia financial assistance grant," I was redirected to many links, such as **this one**.

Here are some at the **national level** —
- **The Leukemia & Lymphoma Society (LLS)**: LLS offers financial assistance to **blood cancer patients** to help with treatment-related expenses, transportation, and copays.
  - Find **local** funds by **state here**
  - More **cancer-related** sources for financial assistance
- **PAN Foundation**: The Patient Access Network (PAN) Foundation provides financial assistance to underinsured patients with **chronic, life-threatening, or rare diseases**. They offer grants to help with out-of-pocket medical expenses.
- **Family Reach**: Family Reach provides financial assistance to families facing the financial burden of **cancer treatment**. They offer grants to help with living expenses and medical costs.
- **The HealthWell Pediatric Assistance Fund**: This fund provides financial assistance to families **with children** who have **chronic or life-altering** medical conditions. They offer grants to help with medical expenses and treatments.
- **Breast Cancer Foundations**: various organizations that cater to those with **breast cancer** patients provide financial assistance.
- **Patient Services Incorporated (PSI)**: PSI provides financial assistance to individuals with **chronic and rare diseases** to help with insurance premiums and medical expenses.
- **American Kidney Fund (AKF)**: AKF offers financial assistance to **kidney patients** to help with treatment costs, transportation, and other related expenses. To apply, contact AKF for more information.

Online Tools for Disabled Students

Microsoft Immersive Reader:

As highlighted in a <u>**video**</u> on my Instagram account, Microsoft has a feature called "Immersive Reader." It can especially be helpful for those who struggle with focusing on long and dense text which is oftentimes required to read in college textbooks.

Bionic Reading:

There is also what's called **bionic reading**, an innovative method that I personally use. This method:

- Increases my reading speed
- Improves my comprehension of what I am reading
- And personalizes how I read long text

For instance: **he**re is **an exam**ple **of wh**at **Bi**onic **re**ading **m**ay **lo**ok **li**ke.

As you can see, it hyper-fixates on certain letters in text to guide your eyes along. Bionic reading is mainly marketed towards neurodivergent people (such as those on the autism spectrum, with dyslexia, ADHD, etc.); **however**, both neurodivergent and neurotypical people have reported how useful it is.

There are various apps, websites, and **free extensions** online for you to try it out such as via Google Chrome, Firefox, and other web browsers.

Accessible Books:

- <u>**Bookshare**</u> makes reading easier. People with dyslexia, blindness, and other reading barriers can customize their experience to suit their learning style.
- <u>**National Library Service (NLS)**</u> is a free braille and talking book library service for people with temporary or permanent low vision, blindness, or a physical, perceptual, or reading disability that prevents them from using regular print materials.

For 50 more tools for students with disabilities, refer to <u>**this blog**</u> post. It organizes the recommendations by **disability type** such as for dyslexia, speech disabilities, hearing impairments, autism, physical, and more!

Moving into Housing with Disabilities

Moving in general can be an exciting time, but it may also present unique challenges for college-level students with disabilities. Here are some tips to make the college move-in day smoother.

- **Arrange for Parking**: If you have a disability parking permit, coordinate with the college's parking office to ensure you have accessible parking arrangements on move-in day.
- **Contact Disability Services**: Reach out to the college's disability services office before move-in day to discuss your specific needs and accommodations. They can provide valuable information and assistance during the move-in process.
- **Request Housing Accommodations**: If you require specific housing accommodations, such as an accessible room or proximity to certain facilities, make these requests well in advance and follow up to ensure they are in place on move-in day.
  - **NOTE**: Sometimes certain dorms or apartments may have mold in them due to being in very old buildings. If this happens to be the case for your room — then request a room change.
  - My cousin had the same experience. Due to his respiratory issues, they were able to accommodate him immediately with a newly renovated room without mold.
- **Plan Ahead for Accessibility**: Familiarize yourself with the campus layout and accessibility features. Know the locations of ramps, elevators, accessible restrooms, and other amenities that will aid your mobility.
- **Pack Essentials Last**: Keep essential items like medications, assistive devices, and important documents in a bag that you carry with you. This way, you'll have everything you need even if moving takes longer than expected.
- **Ask for Help**: Don't hesitate to ask for assistance from family, friends, or college staff during the move-in process. Many colleges have volunteers available to help with moving heavy items or transporting belongings.

- **Take Breaks**: Moving can be physically demanding, so take breaks as needed to rest and recharge. Listen to your body and pace yourself.
- **Prepare for Weather Conditions**: Check the weather forecast for move-in day and dress appropriately. Bring items like umbrellas, hats, or sunscreen if needed.
- **Stay Hydrated and Snack Smartly**: Have water and healthy snacks available to keep your energy up throughout the day.
- **Meet Your Roommate(s)**: If possible, get to know your roommates in advance and communicate any specific needs or preferences you have for shared living space.
- **Orientation and Support Programs**: Participate in orientation and support programs for students with disabilities. They can provide valuable information and connect you with other students in similar situations.
- **Explore Campus Resources**: Familiarize yourself with other campus resources, such as accessible transportation services, counseling centers, and health clinics.

It is also important to know beforehand if the dorm or apartment has an **elevator**. Older housing accommodations may not have them, and of course, going up and down stairs on move-in day can be very exhausting. *Even more so if you live in a hot state like me like — Texas. So, bring PLENTY of water bottles!*

Additionally, determine whether rooms have **adjustable ACs** (rather than ones you cannot adjust) or at least built-in ceiling fans. If not, then it's time for you to buy a fan for yourself!

Finally, consider **working in housing** like I did! It fully paid for my housing, meal plan, and gave me a monthly stipend. As a resident assistant — or **RA** for short — I only really worked 10% of the time since it was more so a "stand-by" job, meaning, I was mainly needed in the case of emergencies which were rare. Of course, how much you work, and the specific benefits included depend on your school, the residence hall you are assigned to, and so forth. So, make sure to **attend interest meetings** in the **fall semester** to learn more about what you can expect regarding the job and the application for it.

Helpful Creators to Follow

As a content creator myself, I wanted to highlight some creators you should consider learning from in the following spaces:

- Disability
- Healthcare
- Personal Finance
- Technology

@PowerfullyIsa: Isabel Mavrides-Calderón is a disability rights activist whose work focuses on advocating for policy change, accessibility, and anti-ableism. She was featured on Teen Vogue 21 under 21 and various other news outlets. Isabel is active on; TikTok and Instagram.

- **Post highlight**: In **this post**, she highlighted the comments she received from students with disabilities during emergency drills and real emergencies. The responses — were shocking.

@AutieNelle: Lauren Melissa Ellzey is an autistic self-advocate, social justice influencer, and fiction author. Through writing and presenting, she seeks to cultivate acceptance for the neurodivergent community. Lauren is active on; Instagram and Twitter (X).

@Crutches_and_Spice: Imani Barbarin is a disability rights activist, communications manager, and writer who has cerebral palsy. She often talks about the intersectionality of being disabled, debunking myths and misinformation about those with disabilities, and more. Imani is active on; Instagram, TikTok, and Twitter (X).

@JoelBervell: Known online as the "Medical Mythbuster," Joel is committed to fighting health disparities in medicine through education and regularly shares topics about racial disparities / biases in healthcare. Joel is active on; Instagram, TikTok, and LinkedIn.

- **Post highlight:** In this **viral post**, he shared how different medical conditions look on different skin tones. Oftentimes certain conditions can go undiagnosed for those with darker skin tones. As seen within this **research study** it found that medical textbook imagery had only 4.5% of dark skin represented, and another **study** — specifically analyzing dermatology textbooks — found that only 4-18% of textbooks had images of dark skin.

@ErikaNKullberg: Erika Kullberg is a lawyer and personal finance creator. Her videos highlight how to save and make money in various ways. Erika covers how to and breaks down the legal terms and conditions of top companies that outline how customers may be entitled to receive compensation. Erika is active on; Instagram, TikTok, YouTube, and has a podcast.

@GigiTheFirstGenMentor: Giovanna Gonzalez is also a personal finance creator. However, she especially focuses on the topic from the first-generation perspective as a child of immigrant parents. She discusses how to manage finances with family in mind and the ways in which cultural values play a role in how financial literacy is perceived and received. Giovanna is active on; Instagram, TikTok, and LinkedIn.

@Teneikaashh You: Teneika Askew's content focuses on sharing resources to upskill and pivot into tech. The tech field can be one of the best industries to work in if you have a disability and these roles are oftentimes remote and high-paying. Teneika is primarily active on; Twitter (X).

@SineadBovell: Sinéad Bovell is a futurist and United Nations speaker. She analyzes how technology currently is and will continue to impact the future. It is important to stay on top of the ever-changing landscape of technology and how these changes may affect those with disabilities. Sinéad is active on; Instagram, TikTok, and YouTube.

Sign the Petition

Do you believe in a future where applying for federal disability services is more accessible and user-friendly to fill out applications? We do too! Join us in our mission to streamline them, making it just as seamless and efficient as the FAFSA.

Sign our petition and stand up for a more inclusive and equitable tomorrow for those with disabilities.

Your signature counts and will help pave the way for positive change in the lives of countless individuals.

[Link to Petition]

Share this petition with your friends, family, and networks to amplify our impact!

#EnableTheDisabled

Let's make history together!

Take the Survey

Calling all individuals who recently discovered Vocational Rehabilitation (VR) and the Workforce Innovation and Opportunity Act (WIOA) through us or externally!

[Link to Survey]

Here are the FACTS:

VR has existed since the Rehabilitation Act of 1973, so about five decades, 50 years.

WIOA has existed since the Workforce Innovation and Opportunity Act (WIOA) was signed into law in 2014 and became effective in 2015, so nearly a decade. Yet many are just now learning about one or both of these programs overall.

Here are the STATS:

According to the National Center for Education Statistics (**NCES**), about 19% of undergraduate students report having a disability.

A research **study** titled *Above-Average Student Loan Debt for Students with Disabilities Attending Postsecondary Institutions* found that "The average federal student loan debt among graduates with disabilities is approximately $27,490."

And according to **StudentAid.gov** their *Federal Student Aid Portfolio Summary* reported that 43.6 million Americans have federal student loans as of 2023.

Here's the IMPACT:

Specifically for VR, (*that caters to those with disabilities as it relates to employment*) — many students who have loan debt could have qualified for the program had they at least known about it and applied.

And with WIOA (*which caters to both individuals with or without disabilities as it relates to employment*) many students in general could have potentially had less student loan debt.

By sharing your experience, you can help us gauge the effectiveness of the government's efforts in spreading awareness about these critical programs. In the survey, you will:

- Answer questions about how you learned about VR and WIOA
- Evaluate the outreach methods you found most helpful
- Contribute to understanding the impact of awareness campaigns

Take the Survey Now! Your feedback will guide us in improving government outreach to ensure that more individuals can access the support they need. Together, we can make a difference in promoting inclusive opportunities for everyone.

[Link to Survey]

Share the survey with others!

Your participation can make a significant impact!

Survey results / research findings will later be shown using the same link above.

Contact Info

Was this information helpful? Did you find info that needs updating?

Then let me know by emailing me at: **Carlynn@scholarship-guru.com**
Also, feel free to leave a **tip here** to get me a coffee or boba tea as a token of appreciation! This helps my productivity a lot by researching and creating even more resources for you guys. ^_^

NOTE: If you have **questions relating to VR or WIOA or any other government resource** — the best course of action **isn't to ask me**, but to ask your local VR counselor or WIOA case manager, etc., because policies, laws, and facts vary depending on where you are and are subject to change from the date of which this book was published.

Regarding scholarships and other forms of financial aid, if you need personalized help, feel free to check out my **services** on my website.

Finally, I also do **speaking engagements!** If you would like for me to speak and teach in-person or virtually at your **school, organization, conference,** etc., — then please use this link **here.**

Social media accounts:
- YouTube: **@ESPdaniella**
- TikTok: **@ESPdaniella**
- Instagram: **@Carle100**
- LinkedIn: **@CarlynnGreene**

Reference Info

Use this **link** or the **QR code above** to access the master document of all links mentioned.
- **Instructions**: Make sure you are signed into your Google account. From there, press the blue button that says, **"Make a copy."**
- Within this document, you will also find additional references not hyperlinked in the book that I used during my research.

The Scholarship Algorithm

You probably remember me mentioning my program and book titled, *The Scholarship Algorithm* which details my step-by-step winning process to obtaining 30x scholarships between undergraduate and graduate school. Many students have won using these resources such as full rides for graduate school, $103,000 in scholarships, $246,000 in scholarships — and even college seniors winning enough to graduate just in time and be debt-free.

"What all is within the book and program?" Read **free previews** of both and **winner testimonials:**
- **Book**: Both digital and print book options available
- **Program**: Use code for 25% off: 25OFFTSA
  - *(**NOTE**: The code includes the letter "o" not zero 0)*

*"What are the **differences** between the program vs. the book?"*
- To learn, refer to this **link**
- **Summary**: With the **book** you are **5x** more likely to win scholarships, and with the **program** you are **10x** more likely.

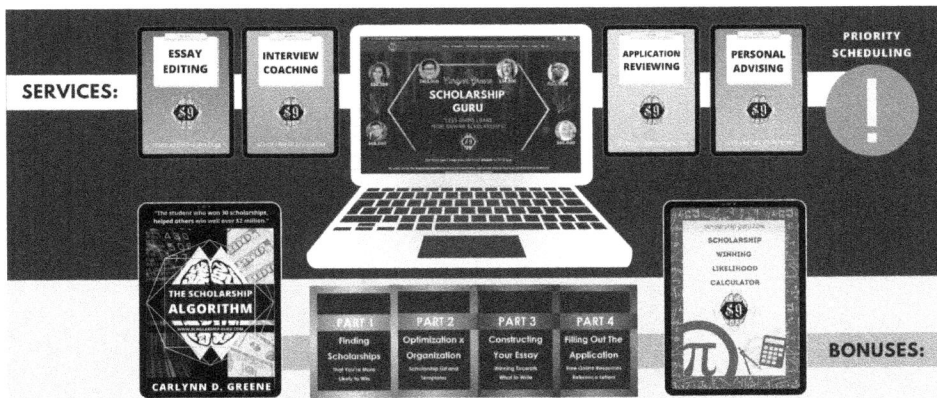

"Why should I study the book or program?"
Scholarships are ***very*** competitive. Every year, thousands of students apply for dozens and hundreds of scholarships — ***but never win***. What many don't realize is that you have to be ***strategic*** with the types of scholarships you apply to and with ***how you convey your message*** within your overall application.

Many people *depend on their stats* (like their GPA, test scores, etc.) to get scholarships, but countless students have that as well. You need *other ways to stand out.*

With my book and program, I teach you the *psychology* behind winning.

Think of applying for scholarships as *marketing yourself.* You have to know how to use *persuasive language,* and really be *memorable* out of the hundreds if not thousands competing against you!

In conclusion, with my **book**, you are **5x more** likely to win and **10x more** likely to win with the **program**.

Both can also potentially help with **other competitive applications** you submit such as for college admissions, internships, and grants.

Of course, there is not a guarantee that you will win — but at least your chances of winning will be significantly higher than they were before learning from the material provided!

Learn more about these resources and others I have on my website: **scholarship-guru.com**

www.ingramcontent.com/pod-product-compliance
Lightning Source LLC
Chambersburg PA
CBHW051756200326
41597CB00025B/4578